World Heritage Wilderness
From the Wrangells to Glacier Bay

By George Matz

ALASKA GEOGRAPHIC® Volume 26, Number 2

To teach many more to better know and more wisely use our natural resources

EDITOR
Penny Rennick

ASSOCIATE EDITOR
Rosanne Pagano

PRODUCTION DIRECTOR
Kathy Doogan

MARKETING DIRECTOR
Jill S. Brubaker

BOOKKEEPER/DATABASE MANAGER
Claire Whitefield

OFFICE ASSISTANT
Melanie Britton

POSTMASTER:
Send address changes to:

ALASKA GEOGRAPHIC®
P.O. Box 93370
Anchorage, Alaska 99509-3370

PRINTED IN U.S.A.

COLOR SEPARATIONS: Graphic Chromatics

PRINTING: Hart Press

ISBN: 1-56661-045-1

PRICE TO NON-MEMBERS THIS ISSUE: $21.95

COVER: *Kluane National Park in the fall evokes images of virgin wildlands, hallmark of this World Heritage Site, the largest protected wilderness on earth. (Mario Villeneuve)*

PREVIOUS PAGE: *Alpenglow highlights the Lakina Valley and Fireweed Mountain in the Wrangells. (Cross Fox Photography)*

FACING PAGE: *Increasing demand for recreation has spawned commercial outfitters such as Howard Mozen's Copper Oar rafting company in McCarthy. (George Wuerthner)*

ALASKA GEOGRAPHIC® (ISSN 0361-1353) is published quarterly by The Alaska Geographic Society, 639 West International Airport Rd., Unit 38, Anchorage, AK 99518. Periodicals postage paid at Anchorage, Alaska, and additional mailing offices. Copyright © 1999 The Alaska Geographic Society. All rights reserved. Registered trademark: Alaska Geographic, ISSN 0361-1353; key title Alaska Geographic. This issue published June 1999.

THE ALASKA GEOGRAPHIC SOCIETY is a non-profit, educational organization dedicated to improving geographic understanding of Alaska and the North, putting geography back in the classroom and exploring new methods of teaching and learning.

MEMBERS RECEIVE *ALASKA GEOGRAPHIC®*, a high-quality, colorful quarterly that devotes each issue to monographic, in-depth coverage of a specific northern region or resource-oriented subject. Back issues are also available. Membership is $49 ($59 to non-U.S. addresses) per year. To order or to request a free catalog of back issues, contact: Alaska Geographic Society, P.O. Box 93370, Anchorage, AK 99509-3370; phone (907) 562-0164 or toll free (888) 255-6697, fax (907) 562-0479, e-mail: akgeo@akgeo.com, web: www.akgeo.com

SUBMITTING PHOTOGRAPHS: Those interested in submitting photos for possible publication should write for a list of upcoming topics or other photo needs and a copy of our editorial guidelines. We cannot be responsible for unsolicited submissions. Submissions not accompanied by sufficient postage for return by certified mail will be returned by regular mail.

CHANGE OF ADDRESS: The post office will not automatically forward *ALASKA GEOGRAPHIC®* when you move. To ensure continuous service, please notify us at least six weeks before moving. Send your new address and membership number or a mailing label from a recent issue of *ALASKA GEOGRAPHIC®* to: Alaska Geographic Society, Box 93370, Anchorage, AK 99509. If your book is returned to us by the post office because it is for some reason undeliverable, we will contact you to ask if you wish to receive a replacement for a small fee to cover additional postage.

The Library of Congress has cataloged this serial publication as follows:

Alaska Geographic. v.1-
    [Anchorage, Alaska Geographic Society] 1972-
    v. ill. (part col.). 23 x 31 cm.
    Quarterly
    Official publication of The Alaska Geographic Society.
    Key title: Alaska geographic, ISSN 0361-1353.

    1. Alaska—Description and travel—1959-
    —Periodicals. I. Alaska Geographic Society.
F901.A266   917.98'04'505   72-92087
Library of Congress 75[79112] MARC-S.

ABOUT THIS ISSUE:
Capturing the overpowering magnificence of the largest protected wilderness in the world has required the knowledge and support of the many scientists who have explored this World Heritage Site in detail. For their help in providing information and/or reviewing portions of the text, George Matz, author of this issue, thanks in particular: from Glacier Bay National Park and Preserve, Mary Beth Moss, resource manager, Carolyn Elder, biologist, Rusty Yerxa, biologist; from Wrangell-St. Elias National Park and Preserve, Jon Jarvis, park superintendent, Danny Rosenkrans, geologist, Carl Mitchell, biologist; from Tatshenshini-Alsek Wilderness Provincial Park, Gordon McCrae, park warden; from Kluane National Park, Lloyd Freese, park warden; and from the Alaska Natural Heritage Program, Keith Boggs and Rob Lipkin.

Editor's note: Because the World Heritage Site is an international wilderness, this book is designed to accommodate both U.S. and Canadian readers. Consequently, the staff has endeavored to provide statistics in both standard U.S. usage and in metric. Also, in a few cases U.S. and Canadian terms for a place are slightly different. For instance, The Icefield Range is the U.S. term, Icefield Ranges is the Canadian term for the core of the St. Elias Mountains. One final item, words in **boldface** type denote glossary entries. ∎

Contents

In A Class By Itself 4

    What Is a World Heritage Site 7

A Wilderness Landscape 8

    North America's Highest Mountains 11

The Land of Living Geology 12

    A Landscape of Living Geology 15

    At A Glance 20

On the Other Side of the Mountains 28

A Crossroads for Vegetation 36

    The Coastal Rain Forest 38

    The Interior Boreal Forest 40

Wood Frogs to Whales 52

    Wetlands 59

    Phantom of the Forest 69

The First People 76

Western Explorers Arrive 86

The Adventurers 92

    Master of Big Water 100

    Guardian of Long Lake 104

So You Want To Visit 106

Glossary 109

Bibliography 110

Index 110

In A Class By Itself

FACING PAGE:

Named for well-known naturalist-explorer John Muir, Muir Inlet branches off the east side of Glacier Bay and extends 47 miles to Muir and Riggs glaciers. (Laurent Dick)

My first excursion to the Wrangell-St. Elias mountains occurred in July 1959 when I was a 17-year-old kid, freshly graduated from a suburban Chicago high school. A buddy and I decided we would spend the summer in Alaska before we started college. We had big ideas about adventure and making lots of money. We were right about the adventure but had to call home for money to afford the trip back.

One of the strongest memories I have of this Huckleberry-Finn-type journey was my first airplane ride from Chitina on the Copper River south to Tebay Lakes, now within Wrangell-St. Elias National Park. I flew into this pair of beautiful mountain lakes to visit a rustic camp and spend a couple of days fishing from a leaky rowboat. As the floatplane took off and climbed into the clear sky, the bush pilot told me to look to the left and take in the grandeur of the "world's largest icefield" that covered Mount Wrangell. While this wasn't exactly correct (it isn't the largest icefield), it didn't matter. I was amazed. So much ice and so many big mountains. I knew then that this was a special place.

As you get older, you learn more about a lot of things you already knew. Now, nearly 40 years later and after numerous hiking, skiing, kayaking, canoeing and rafting trips in the Wrangell-St. Elias region, after having lived in the three climatic zones that determine the region's weather, and after studying the natural history of Alaska for more than 20 years, I am reassured that my first impression on seeing the icefield was right: This is a special place. In fact, now that I better understand some of the natural forces that have shaped this landscape, I think the vast area covered by the Wrangell-St. Elias Mountains is sacred. The region is too powerful, too dynamic and too undisturbed by humans to be compared to anywhere else. It is in a class by itself.

One difference from my first visit is that the region is now officially recognized as a special place. The mountains are now protected by four large parks: Wrangell-St. Elias National Park and Preserve and Glacier Bay National Park and Preserve in Alaska, Kluane National Park and Reserve in the Yukon and Tatshenshini-Alsek Wilderness Provincial Park in British Columbia. To further recognize the area's uniqueness, all four parks are now one Natural World Heritage Site totaling more than 24 million acres (9.6 million ha), the largest contiguous expanse of protected land in the world. In addition to these four jewels, several smaller gems, such as the Alaska Chilkat Bald Eagle Preserve near Haines and the Copper River Delta Critical Habitat Area near Cordova, flank this world heritage wilderness.

This Natural World Heritage Site deserves its international recognition and protection. It is

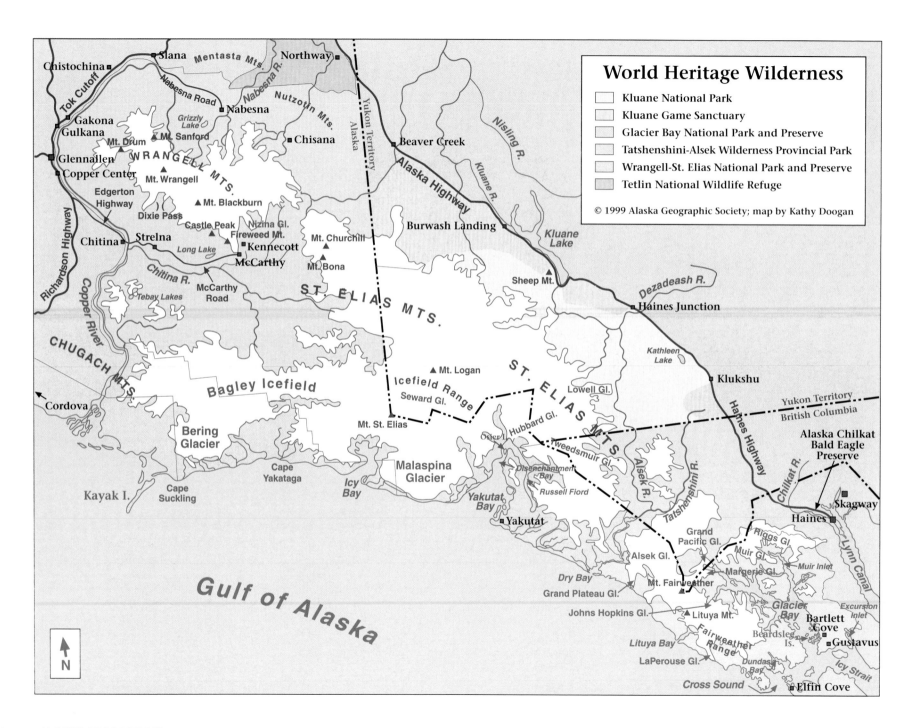

World Heritage Wilderness

- Kluane National Park
- Kluane Game Sanctuary
- Glacier Bay National Park and Preserve
- Tatshenshini-Alsek Wilderness Provincial Park
- Wrangell-St. Elias National Park and Preserve
- Tetlin National Wildlife Refuge

© 1999 Alaska Geographic Society; map by Kathy Doogan

Chistochina • Slana • Mentasta Mts. • Northway
Tok Cutoff • Nabesna Road • Nabesna R. • Nutzotin Mts. • Yukon Territory Alaska
Gakona • Gulkana • Grizzly Lake • Mt. Sanford • Chisana • Beaver Creek
Mt. Drum • WRANGELL MTS. • Alaska Highway • Nisling R. • Kluane R.
Glennallen • Copper Center • Mt. Wrangell
Edgerton Highway • Mt. Blackburn
Dixie Pass • Castle Peak • Nizina Gl. • Fireweed Mt. • Burwash Landing • Kluane Lake
Chitina • Strelna • Long Lake • Kennecott • Mt. Churchill
McCarthy • Mt. Bona • Sheep Mt.
Chitina R. • McCarthy Road • ST. ELIAS MTS.
Richardson Highway • Copper River • Tebay Lakes • Dezadeash R.
CHUGACH MTS. • Haines Junction
Mt. Logan • Kathleen Lake
Bagley Icefield • Icefield Range • Seward Gl. • ST. ELIAS MTS. • Lowell Gl. • Klukshu
Cordova • Mt. St. Elias • Yukon Territory British Columbia
Bering Glacier • Oster I. • Hubbard Gl. • Haines Highway
Cape Yakataga • Malaspina Glacier • Tweedsmuir Gl. • Alaska Chilkat Bald Eagle Preserve
Icy Bay • Disenchantment Bay • Alsek R. • Chilkat R.
Kayak I. • Cape Suckling • Russell Fiord • Yakutat Bay • Skagway
Yakutat • Haines
Grand Pacific Gl. • Riggs Gl. • Lynn Canal
Dry Bay • Alsek Gl. • Muir Gl. • Muir Inlet
Grand Plateau Gl. • Mt. Fairweather • Margerie Gl.
Johns Hopkins Gl. • Lituya Mt. • Glacier Bay • Excursion Inlet
Gulf of Alaska • Fairweather Range • Beardslee Is. • Bartlett Cove • Gustavus
Lituya Bay • Dundas Bay • Icy Strait
LaPerouse Gl. • Cross Sound • Elfin Cove

N

a place to observe nature on its terms. The human presence on this landscape has been slight; the biggest changes in recent times have been caused not by people but by massive geologic forces and dynamic ecological succession. Whether you expect to personally experience this sacred place or just be satisfied in knowing that it exists, you can be assured that the land is protected now and into the future. So follow me on a journey through the natural and cultural history of this remote and wonderful corner of the world. ▲

What Is a World Heritage Site?

A World Heritage Site has outstanding cultural or natural values that are being preserved or protected by the nation in which the site is located. The site is either a historically significant example of human endeavor (Independence Hall in Philadelphia) or an impressive sample of nature's grandeur (Grand Canyon National Park for its geology and Everglades National Park for its biology). World Heritage Sites are considered a common heritage for all people, and are intended to bring closer cooperation among nations and worldwide recognition of the cultural and natural values of a special place.

Some critics have claimed that allowing a place to become a World Heritage Site is tantamount to turning the property over to the United Nations, thereby giving up local control. While being on the list is intended to emphasize the conservation of a site rather than its development, neither the United Nations nor UNESCO exerts any legal control over actual management of the site. Submitting an application to the World Heritage Committee, which designates the site, and implementing an acceptable conservation plan for a site is a voluntary effort chosen by the respective nation. Listing does give the site international recognition, thereby providing greater awareness of threats from development.

The concept of World Heritage Sites originated during Richard Nixon's administration. An international initiative launched by the United States soon led to an agreement that was adopted by the General Conference of the United Nations Educational, Scientific and Cultural Organization (UNESCO) in 1972. The Convention Concerning the Protection of the World Cultural and Natural Heritage was ratified by the U.S. Senate, and the United States became the first nation to sign the agreement. To date, more than 156 nations have agreed to participate in the program.

In early 1999, the World Heritage List included 582 sites in 114 nations. The United States has eight cultural and 10 natural sites, Canada has five cultural and five natural sites, and there are two joint U.S/Canada natural sites. To be selected for the World Heritage List, a site must:

1. be an outstanding example of major stages of earth's history; or

2. be an outstanding example of significant ongoing ecological and biological processes in the evolution and development of terrestrial, fresh water, coastal and marine ecosystems and communities of plants and animals; or

3. contain superlative natural phenomena or areas of exceptional natural beauty and aesthetic importance; or

4. contain the most important and significant natural habitat for in-situ conservation of biological diversity.

In chronological order, Kluane National Park and Reserve, Wrangell-St. Elias National Park and Preserve, Glacier Bay National Park and Preserve and Tatshenshini-Alsek Wilderness Provincial Park have each been designated a Natural World Heritage Site. Because the four parks are contiguous, they are now considered one collective site. The World Heritage Committee has suggested there be a distinct single name for this site, but none has yet emerged. ■

A Wilderness Landscape

The Wrangell and St. Elias mountains form a sweeping arc of towering peaks and sprawling glaciers that parallels the Pacific Coast for nearly 500 miles (800 km). Immediately to the southwest and north rise two sibling mountain groups, the Chugach and Nutzotins. This family of mountain ranges straddles two regions of Alaska, part of the Yukon and a corner of British Columbia, covering an area nearly as large as Nepal. Scenic grandeur and spectacular examples of geological and biological change and contrast, not mere size, make the Wrangell-St. Elias-Glacier Bay wilderness an extraordinary testament to the physical and biological artistry of nature.

The base of this mountain barrier begins near sea level; its tallest ramparts embrace 17 of the 30 highest peaks in North America. Incredibly, all 17 are higher than California's Mount Whitney, at 14,494-foot (4,396 m) the tallest peak in the Lower 48. The St. Elias Mountains are not only the highest coastal mountains in the world, but have a vertical relief greater than the Himalayas. To compare, Mount Everest (29,028 ft/8,805 m), the world's tallest peak, sits atop the 15,000-foot (4,550 m) Tibetan Plateau. But Mount Logan in the St. Elias Mountains rises 19,545 feet (5,929 m) and its base begins near sea level only 40 miles (64 km) inland from the Gulf of Alaska coast.

The region's glaciers and icefields number in the hundreds and are just as spectacular as its peaks, routinely claiming superlatives such as largest and longest. Here lies the most extensive array of glaciers and icefields in the world, outside of Antarctica and Greenland. The Bagley Icefield in the Chugach Mountains is the largest on the continent, Bering is the largest glacier and Malaspina the largest piedmont glacier. At 75 miles (120 km) Nabesna is the world's longest glacier excluding those in Antarctica and Greenland. Some glaciers, such as Hubbard, begin at high elevations, wind down U-shaped valleys as slow rivers of ice, and eventually break apart at tidewater, depositing a steady flow of icebergs into nearby fiords. This movement of glaciers has fashioned a stark, unforgettable landscape that is increasingly attracting visitors.

The extensive mountains and glaciers create not only their own weather, but also divide contrasting extremes in climate. The coastal side of the Wrangell and St. Elias mountains has a maritime climate with relatively mild temperatures, many cloudy days, considerable precipitation and sometimes hurricane force winds. Pacific-facing slopes of Mount St. Elias (18,008 ft/5,462 m) may be the wettest place on earth. Conversely, the region's interior flank has a continental climate with long, clear, cold winters. Summer days tend to be warm and

This cluster of paintbrush brightens the banks of the Lower Alsek River. Paintbrush (Castilleja species) comes in several colors and has adapted to a variety of habitats. At least one of the nine species of this plant can be found throughout most of Alaska and northern Canada. (George Matz)

RIGHT:

Mountain goats forage highland meadows above Lowell Glacier in Kluane National Park. (Michael Speaks)

sunny at lower elevations and precipitation is low, comparable in some areas to a desert.

The extremes in topography and climate result in diverse fauna and flora. Wet conditions on the coastal side nourish a temperate rain forest, dominated by Sitka spruce and western hemlock. The land and marine animals that thrive here are much the same as those found in Southeast Alaska. Across the mountains, the climate fosters a boreal forest with a mix of white spruce and birch. Animals inhabiting in this forest, such as moose and caribou, typify the subarctic. Swinging southeast from the Wrangells to British Columbia, the spruce/birch forest gives way to a Rocky-Mountain-type of forest with lodgepole pine and subalpine fir. An alpine belt of rock and ice harboring some surprising life forms such as algae and iceworms separates the two forest types.

Native Americans have inhabited this area for thousands of years, even before the most

recent ice age. Their food, shelter, cultures and modes of transportation blended well with the mountains, glaciers, waters, forests, fish and wildlife. The differences in the cultures of the Tlingits, Athabaskans and Eyaks coincided with the diverse environments found in the region.

In 1741, Vitus Bering led the first major European expedition to explore the North Pacific. The first land they saw in North America was Mount St. Elias. Despite this early discovery, Western culture has trod gently on the region. Century-old gold rushes and later copper mining ventures spawned short-lived settlements such as Chisana. All that remains of this pioneer activity are a few small towns scattered mostly on the fringe of the mountains, some abandoned mills and a few gravel roads.

Today, outdoor adventurers and tourists fill the gap left by the miners. This country is becoming internationally known for its mountain climbing, river rafting, sea kayaking, fishing, hunting and wildlife watching, activities nourished by this unparalleled international wilderness. Only the cruise ships that ply Glacier Bay, Yakutat Bay and the Gulf of Alaska bring the accouterments of modern urban civilization to this outpost of nature.

Most of the land here is publicly owned and lies within the four parks. The future of the area depends on a management policy that protects the natural and cultural heritage while allowing compatible uses and furthering scientific understanding of the geological and biological attributes of the land. Not an easy job, given competing demands, but one that is essential if future generations are to enjoy the heritage we now cherish. ▲

North America's Highest Mountains

NOTE: Bold type indicates peaks within the World Heritage Site. Officially, the Wrangell and St. Elias mountains have 17 of the 30 highest peaks in North America. Yet if all the high peaks in this mountain complex had names, the number would be higher. For instance, Mount Blackburn (16,390 ft/4,972 m) has a second peak 16,286 feet (4,940 m) high that would be tied with Mount Kennedy as the 13th highest peak in North America if it were separately recognized.

	NAME	PLACE	MT. RANGE	HEIGHT (FT./M.)
1.	McKinley	Alaska	Alaska	20,320/6,164
2.	**Logan**	**Yukon**	**Icefield**	**19,545/5,929**
3.	Citlaltepec	Mexico	Occidental	18,700/5,672
4.	**St. Elias**	**Alaska-Yukon**	**Icefield**	**18,008/5,462**
5.	Popocatepetl	Mexico	Occidental	17,887/5,426
6.	Foraker	Alaska	Alaska	17,400/5,278
7.	Iztaccihuatl	Mexico	Occidental	17,343/5,261
8.	**Lucania**	**Yukon**	**Icefield**	**17,147/5,201**
9.	**King**	**Yukon**	**Icefield**	**16,971/5,148**
10.	**Steele**	**Yukon**	**Icefield**	**16,644/5,049**
11.	**Bona**	**Alaska**	**St. Elias**	**16,550/5,020**
12.	**Blackburn**	**Alaska**	**Wrangell**	**16,390/4,972**
13.	**Kennedy**	**Yukon**	**Icefield**	**16,286/4,940**
14.	**Sanford**	**Alaska**	**Wrangell**	**16,237/4,925**
15.	South Buttress	Alaska	Alaska	15,885/4,818
16.	**Wood**	**Yukon**	**Icefield**	**15,885/4,818**
17.	**Vancouver**	**Alaska-Yukon**	**Icefield**	**15,700/4,762**
18.	**Churchill**	**Alaska**	**St. Elias**	**15,638/4,743**
19.	**Fairweather**	**Alaska-Yukon**	**Fairweather**	**15,300/4,641**
20.	Zinantecatl	Mexico	Occidental	15,016/4,555
21.	**Hubbard**	**Alaska-Yukon**	**Icefield**	**15,015/4,554**
22.	**Bear**	**Alaska**	**St. Elias**	**14,831/4,499**
23.	**Walsh**	**Yukon**	**Icefield**	**14,780/4,483**
24.	East Buttress	Alaska	Alaska	14,730/4,468
25.	Matlalcueyetl	Mexico	Occidental	14,636/4,439
26.	Hunter	Alaska	Alaska	14,573/4,420
27.	**Alverstone**	**Alaska-Yukon**	**Icefield**	**14,5654,418**
28.	Browne Tower	Alaska	Alaska	14,530/4,407
29.	Whitney	California	Sierra Nevada	14,494/4,396
30.	Elbert	Colorado	Sawatch	14,433/4,378

Source: *The World Almanac® and Book of Facts 1994*, except for Mt. Logan whose elevation is the result of a 1992 expedition undertaken specifically to measure the mountain.

The Land of Living Geology

Geological processes seem as stable as the Rock of Gibraltar, at least within the typical life span of a human. But in the geologically active Wrangell, St. Elias and Chugach mountains, the accelerated movements of mountains and glaciers bring perceptible changes to the landscape within a generation or less. Here, geology comes alive.

Some geological events happen abruptly, such as a powerful earthquake that literally moves mountains several feet within a matter of minutes. Other changes are subtle but persistent, the advance and retreat of glaciers for instance, and require a few years or decades to significantly alter the landscape.

While other places might have earthquakes or glaciers, few can match the variety and complexity of geological processes occurring in this region. Even among locations that are geologically active, the Wrangell, St. Elias and Chugach mountains stand out because of their massive scale and rapid rate of change.

Here two geologic superpowers, **plate tectonics** and glaciation, meet with unusual intensity to create opposite results. Their coming together is a complimentary, not a conflicting action, like a yin-yang relationship on the grandest scale. Plate tectonics has the power to fold, uplift and break the earth's crust, spawning mountain ranges; glaciation has the strength to mold the earth's surface, wearing down what has been built up. Each of these forces is powerful enough separately to make or remake the shape and size of continents.

Plate tectonics refers to the continuous motion of the earth's land masses that are riding on great plates of the earth's crust. These plates are composed of different rocks, and in general, oceanic plates are heavier than continental plates. The theory of plate tectonics helps explain mountain building processes. The collision of the Pacific plate, which covers most of the bottom of the Pacific Ocean, with the North American plate, which includes Canada, the United States, Mexico and some of the Atlantic Ocean floor, has slowly, but with violent outbursts, uplifted and folded the crust of the earth, creating a series of mountain ranges that parallel the Pacific Coast. Uplift reaches its greatest height where these plates collide along the coast of the Gulf of Alaska at the World Heritage Site.

Glaciers are nature's civil engineers. When glaciers retreat, they leave behind a composite of sculpting, such as U-shaped valleys, and deposits, such as **moraines**, that not only control the flow of water, but determine future habitat for flora and fauna. Because the Wrangell, St. Elias and Chugach mountains are impacted both by moisture-laden storms from the Pacific Ocean and cold interior air masses,

FACING PAGE:
Nizina Glacier winds its way out of the Wrangell Mountains in this view from Chitistone Mountain northeast of McCarthy. (Curvin Metzler)

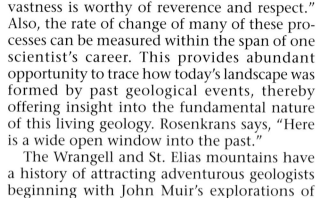

Two natural forces cast a heavy hand over the World Heritage Site, plate tectonics and glaciation. Plate tectonics builds up the land and glaciation carves it away. This world heritage wilderness has outstanding examples of both, such as this pock-marked ice from Gilman Glacier scouring the slopes of the Fairweather Range of the St. Elias Mountains. (Matthew Cahill)

snowfall in coastal areas tends to be extreme. Glaciers and icefields, fed by this snowfall, cover more than half the region. The advance and retreat of these glaciers continues to shape and reshape the landscape.

This combination of tectonics and glaciation fashions spectacular scenery as well as intriguing geology. Danny Rosenkrans, a geologist for Wrangell-St. Elias National Park and Preserve, thinks there is no better place to practice his profession. Geologists consider the present a key to the past. As Rosenkrans points out, "The Wrangell-St. Elias mountains have experienced a wide array of physical phenomena that are not common to many places. Its bewildering

vastness is worthy of reverence and respect." Also, the rate of change of many of these processes can be measured within the span of one scientist's career. This provides abundant opportunity to trace how today's landscape was formed by past geological events, thereby offering insight into the fundamental nature of this living geology. Rosenkrans says, "Here is a wide open window into the past."

The Wrangell and St. Elias mountains have a history of attracting adventurous geologists beginning with John Muir's explorations of Glacier Bay more than a century ago. Between 1879 and 1899, Muir made five trips to Glacier Bay to explore the "ancient glaciers... making new landscapes, scenery, and beauty which so mysteriously influence every human being, and to some extent all life." Though the region's inaccessibility has limited the amount of investigation that has taken place since Muir's explorations, a succession of discoveries has contributed to glacial, plate tectonic and recent global warming theories. While musing over past observations, Rosenkrans says, with a twinkle in his eye, "There are still great scientific and personal discoveries to be made."

The discoveries to be made are not just for professional geologists. Those interested in natural history can observe for themselves this great geologic handshake and ponder how it connects to climate, flora and fauna, and even human development. Since these forces are still active, viewers can speculate how the present is not only a key to the past, but an indication of the future.

Tectonics: The Building Blocks

Two hundred million years ago, the North American plate barely extended as far west as

A LANDSCAPE OF LIVING GEOLOGY

COMPOSITE TERRANE OR TERRANE	SUBDVIDED INTO	WHEN FORMED	WHEN ATTACHED TO ALASKA	FAULT BOUNDARIES	LOCATION	NOTES
Wrangell Composite Terrane			100 MYA*	Denali	Pacific Coast (mostly Wrangell Mts.)	Denali Fault, a major tectonic boundary of North America.
	Alexander Terrane	500 to 66 MYA			St. Elias Mts.	Joined Wrangellia Terrane 200 MYA.
	Wrangellia Terrane	300 MYA				Began within 15° lat. of equator. Fossil record left some of first evidence of plate tectonics.
Southern Margin Composite Terrane				Border Ranges (north); Contact (south)	Baranof Island to Kodiak Island	Among world's largest subduction related accretionary complexes.
	Chugach Terrane	250 to 66 MYA	65 MYA			Counter-clockwise bending of western section formed arc of Gulf of Alaska coast.
	Prince William Terrane					
	Ghost Rocks Terrane					
Yakutat Composite Terrane			26 MYA to present	Queen Charlotte-Fairweather Fault	Offshore from Cross Sound to Copper River Delta	Has slid north about 370 mi. (600 km). Continues moving 2 in. (55 mm) per year. Contributes to uplift of Wrangell, St. Elias and Chugach mountains which continues at 1 in. (2.5 cm) per year.

*MYA = millions of years ago

present-day Alaska. The area where the World Heritage Site is today was ocean. Then huge blocks of the earth's crust, slowly being carried north by the Pacific plate, began attaching to the North American plate, accreting or adding to the continent's land mass in a long series of earth-shattering episodes. These blocks, some as large as midsize states, are called terranes.

Although much of Kluane National Park is ice, snow and rock, the northern and eastern fringe offers beautiful vistas of prime wilderness, such as this image of Kathleen Lake. (George Matz)

Hikers are intrigued by these carbonaceous rocks on Goatherd Mountain in Kluane National Park. (Michael Speaks)

The creation of the Wrangell, St. Elias and Chugach mountains provides some of the world's best examples of this geologic process.

Terranes explain the geological development for much of North America west of the Rocky Mountains. According to a theory first proposed in 1980 by University of Arizona geologist Peter Coney and associates, some of the terranes that accreted to the North American plate originated in the Pacific basin, thousands of miles to the southwest of Alaska. Geologists have since determined that Alaska is made up of about 50 terranes and subterranes with about 20 more in southern Yukon and northwestern British Columbia. Each terrane is bounded by a network of faults.

The origin of individual terranes was unraveled by geologists after detailed examination of fossil records and the magnetic orientation of rock formations. Some terranes contain fossils of marine organisms that inhabited tropical waters long ago. After these organisms were imbedded in rock, they were transported from the South Pacific to the North American coast by the Pacific plate as it drifted to the northeast.

The magnetic orientation of rocks offers additional evidence of terrane origins. When molten rock cools or sediment settles to become rock, the magnetic orientation of its iron-bearing components, such as magnetite, is locked in place. This orientation indicates the latitude of formation of the rock as well as any rotation caused by folding of the rock. Here again, the magnetic alignment of many terranes reveals a tropical origin.

As movement of the Pacific plate ground against the edge of the North American plate, some terranes broke off, accreting to the continental land mass. Other terranes, or parts thereof, continued to drift northward with the Pacific plate. On reaching the Aleutian trench in the ocean south of the Aleutian Islands, the heavier Pacific plate, made of basalt, subducted or sank, uplifting the North American plate. Parts of the terrane, composed of material more

The highest coastal range in the world, the St. Elias Mountains cluster at the top of the Gulf of Alaska, pushed up there by the inexorable force of plate tectonics. Their core, the Icefield Range (Canadians say Ranges) contains the highest average elevation of any group of peaks in North America. (Ed Darack)

Figure 1: The Wrangell-St. Elias area is a classic example of plate tectonics theory, which maintains that the earth's crust is made up of a series of gigantic plates that float on the earth's mantle. Pieces of land, called terranes, are carried on these shifting plates, and when two plates meet, pieces of crust from one plate are attached to another plate. This photo illustrates how the World Heritage Site is made up of a jumble of tectonic terranes. Colors indicate age of the different terranes with the palest colors representing the oldest, the brightest colors the youngest; the heavy solid line shows terrane boundaries; the dot-dash line marks the Alaska-Canada border. The dots within a terrane indicate that unit has been altered by metamorphism. The chicken-feet pattern marks granitic and gneissic rocks and the letters stand for the names of individual terranes, for instance, YA (Yakutat terrane), SE (St. Elias terrane). (Source: "Lithotectonic Terrane Map of Alaska and Adjacent Parts of Canada," by N.J. Silberling, D.L. Jones. J.W.H. Monger, P.J. Coney, H.C. Berg and G. Plafker, in The Geology of Alaska *(1994). Reprinted with permission.)*

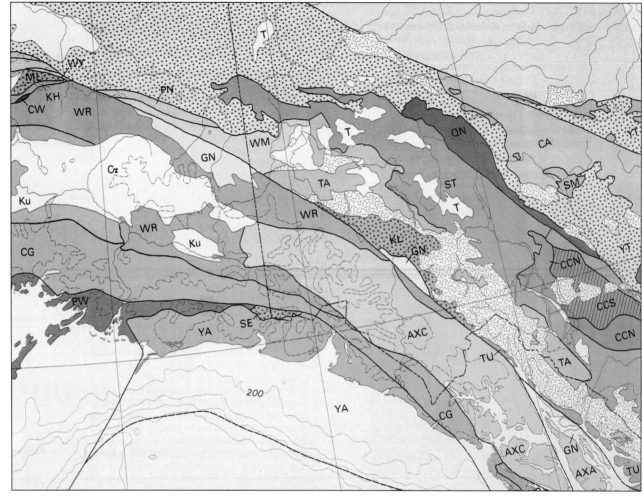

buoyant than basalt, were scraped off and spread along the continental margin, creating a mountain range that now parallels the coast. The subduction of the Pacific plate induced volcanic activity that added to the mountain building.

Beginning about 200 million years ago, the first terrane docked against the North American plate. This was the Yukon-Tanana terrane, which is now the upper part of the Yukon and Tanana river basins just north of the Wrangell and St. Elias mountains. This was also the birth of Alaska, geologically speaking.

As additional terranes drifted north and attached to the North American plate, the land mass that became Alaska, southern Yukon and northwestern British Columbia grew larger. A review of all terranes that contributed to the region is much too complicated to describe here. Figure 1 (at left) indicates the complexity. What simplifies matters is that these terranes combined into one of three composite terranes before accreting to the North American plate: The Wrangellia composite terrane, which now includes both the Wrangell and St. Elias mountains; the Southern Margin composite terrane, which formed the Chugach Mountains and Prince William Sound, and most recently, the Yakutat composite terrane, which is part of the Gulf of Alaska **continental shelf**.

The Wrangellia composite terrane was scraped off as the Pacific plate subducted beneath the North American plate. The folding and faulting from this collision caused uplifting and extensive volcanic activity. During the past 26 million years, thousands of relatively passive lava flows from broad shield volcanoes have created the Wrangell volcanic field, which today covers about 4,000 square miles (10,400 sq km), an area slightly smaller than the state of Connecticut. These volcanoes also created the highest peaks in the Wrangell Mountains, many higher than 10,000 feet (3,033 m). All except Boomerang volcano near Slana have **calderas**.

About 200,000 years ago, faults began to take up some of the stress created by the Pacific plate and the rate of subduction, as well as volcanic activity in the Wrangell Mountains, decreased. Today, Mount Wrangell (14,163 ft/ 4,296 m), the youngest volcano in the range, is the only one considered active. Other examples of volcanism are the mud volcanoes in the Copper River basin near Mount Drum (12,010 ft/3,643 m).

The St. Elias Mountains have not been as volcanically active as the Wrangells, but can claim two of the largest eruptions in North America during the past 2,000 years. Mount Churchill (15,638 ft/4,743 m) blew up about 1,900 years ago and again 1,250 years ago, releasing a total of 12 cubic miles (50 cu km) of volcanic ash over more than 130,000 square miles (338,000 sq km) of eastern Alaska, the Yukon and Northwest Territories. This White River Ash Bed still appears as a light-gray layer of powder just beneath the soil and can often be seen at road cuts on the Alaska Highway.

Because of the ongoing movement and subduction of plates and the linkage of numerous faults, the Wrangell, St. Elias and Chugach mountains are one of the world's

Mineral deposits on the north side of the Wrangell Mountains led to development of placer operations at Chisana, a now mostly abandoned settlement, and of hardrock mines at Nabesna. These buildings are about all that remain of the gold mining project at the end of the Nabesna Road. (Roz Goodman)

AT A GLANCE

SIZE:	**24 million acres** (9.6 million ha). This World Heritage Site is the largest contiguous expanse of protected land in the world.
COMPONENTS:	**Wrangell-St. Elias National Park and Preserve** Size: 13,188,325 acres (5,342,040 ha) **Kluane National Park and Reserve** Size: 5,443,786 acres (2,203,100 ha). In addition, about 1.5 million acres (0.6 million ha) between the park and the Alaska Highway are designated Kluane Game Sanctuary. **Tatshenshini-Alsek Wilderness Provincial Park** Size: 2,367,185 acres (958,000 ha) **Glacier Bay National Park and Preserve** Size: 3,300,000 acres (1,335,510 ha)
HIGHEST POINT:	**Mount Logan in Kluane National Park** At 19,545 feet (5,929 m), Logan is also the highest point in Canada and the second highest in North America. Nearby Mount St. Elias, in Wrangell-St. Elias National Park, is the second highest point in the World Heritage Site, the second highest point in Alaska and the third highest point on the continent at 18,008 feet (5,462 m).
MAJOR RIVERS:	**Copper River**, running from the north side of the Wrangell Mountains 250 miles (400 km) through the Chugach Mountains to the Gulf of Alaska. **Alsek River**, flowing 240 miles (384 km) from Kluane National Park through the St. Elias Mountains to the Gulf of Alaska at Dry Bay.
MAJOR GLACIERS:	**Bering Glacier** and its source, the Bagley Icefield, cover 2,250 square miles (5,850 sq km). The glacier reaches the Gulf of Alaska coast east of the Copper River delta. The Bagley Icefield is the largest in North America, and the Bering complex (glacier and icefield) is larger than the state of Delaware. **Malaspina Glacier**, at the foot of Mount St. Elias, covers 850 square miles (2,210 km). Malaspina, a classic piedmont glacier, is larger than the state of Rhode Island.
TREE LINE:	**Glacier Bay:** Tidewater near glaciers to 2,500 feet (800 m) **Tatshenshini-Alsek:** 3,000 feet (910 m) **Kluane:** 3,500 - 4,000 feet (1,000 - 1,200 m) **Wrangell-St. Elias:** 3,000 - 4,000 feet (900 - 1,200 m)

most seismically active areas. This region has frequent earthquakes, among the largest in recorded history. Approximately 11 percent of the world's earthquakes occur in Alaska. Considering that it has only 0.3 percent of the earth's surface area, Alaska obviously gets more than its share. Although most of the quakes now originate in the Aleutians, between 1899 and 1993 the Yakataga seismic gap, from Glacier Bay to Cape Suckling near the Copper River delta, was the epicenter for more than 100 earthquakes of magnitude 5.0 or greater. Two in 1899 were greater than 8.0. Not far away, Prince William Sound was the epicenter for the infamous 1964 earthquake, which measured 9.2 in moment magnitude, the largest recorded in North America. [**Editor's note:** In the more than 30 years since this earthquake, scientists have revised their measuring systems and no longer use the Richter scale. According to the West Coast and Alaska Tsunami Warning Center in Palmer, 9.2 moment magnitude is the revised measurement for the 1964 quake.]

Some of these earthquakes have instantly changed the local landscape. In June 1958, a quake in Lituya Bay shook loose 40 million cubic yards (30 million cu m) of rock that plunged down steep mountain slopes and crashed into the bay. The displacement of the water caused the highest splash wave ever recorded. The huge wave, moving at about 100 mph, rose 1,720 feet (522 m) up the facing mountainside, wiping out 4 square miles (10 sq km) of forest as well as two out of three fishing boats anchored overnight in the bay.

Landslides caused by weathering rather than earthquakes are also common in the World Heritage Site. The area is so remote that landslides that would be catastrophic in most places aren't even witnessed here. For example, a large landslide occurred January 4, 1993, on the flank of Nelson Mountain several miles east of Chitina. When they investigated, geologists found that the landslide was 2.8 miles (4.5 km) long and 0.7 miles (1.1 km) wide at its toe, which came to rest one-third the way across the flood plain of the Chitina River. The volume of material displaced is estimated to be 4 million cubic yards (3.1 million cu m). The cause appears to be related to steep slopes and a warm period with above-average precipitation and an increased number of freeze-thaw cycles.

While change to the landscape due to movements of the earth is a certainty within the World Heritage Site, what is totally uncertain is when change will occur and at what magnitude. The geology here is a lot like life itself. And like life, changes to the landscape can be interesting and rewarding to explore.

Glaciation: Sculpting the Land

Several periods of glaciation have marked the past 10 million years or so, but unlike the docking of terranes, each period has obliterated much of the record of preceding glaciers. During the **Pleistocene epoch** (the Great Ice Age) which began about 2 million years ago and ended 10,000 to 15,000 years ago, the Wrangell, St. Elias and Chugach mountains were buried beneath a thick, continental ice sheet. Spared glaciation were the interior lowlands of Alaska and the Yukon, an area referred to as **Beringia**.

The continental ice sheet of the Pleistocene was so overwhelming that all the valleys of this world heritage wilderness were filled with

thousands of feet of ice, a barrier that changed the direction of flow of the Alsek, Copper and Yukon rivers. Large lakes were formed north of the mountains, similar to 154-square-mile (400 sq km) Kluane Lake that now exists in the Yukon. The sheet of ice even bulged into the Gulf of Alaska, reaching as far offshore as the continental shelf. Sea level was about 300 feet (91 m) lower then because of the tremendous volume of water stranded above sea level in the form of ice and snow. Bedrock beneath the glaciers was actually compressed by the overbearing weight of ice.

During this time, only mountain peaks and ridges, called nunataks, protruded above the thousands of feet of ice. Nunataks were spared

The rapid advance of Hubbard Glacier at the head Yakutat Bay caught the attention of glaciologists in the mid-1980s, when the glacier overrode Osier Island and blocked Russell Fiord, turning it into a lake. Scientists feared that if the ice dam at the glacier's face didn't break, the water in the lake would back up so high it would overflow its basin and flood the Situk Valley, endangering people in the Yakutat area. In 1986, the dam did break, draining Russell Lake at the rate of 87,400 square yards (69,920 sq m) per second. (Steve McCutcheon)

Rugged ridgelines and glaciers or permanent snowfields mark the Alsek River valley near the British Columbia-Alaska border. (George Matz)

National Park Service coastal mapping technician Bill Eichenlaub correlates survey data sheets with mapping area segments marked on aerial photographs. Glacier Bay staff are performing an extensive baseline inventory of the park's intertidal resources. (Scott Croll)

the scraping by glaciers and retain to this day a more rocky appearance. These rocky islands provided a refuge for some of the few species of fauna and flora that survived the Pleistocene and that would repopulate the land when glaciers receded.

Over time, glaciers come and go. Like frozen seas with long tidal fluctuations, the area covered by glaciers flows back and forth based on what seems to be slight changes in climate. Near the end of the Pleistocene, the climate warmed a few degrees and the glaciers began retreating, but with relatively short, intermittent advances.

During the **Holocene epoch**, our current period, the climate cooled four times and glaciers once again advanced. The most recent advance is called the Little Ice Age, which began about 500 years ago and tapered off about 1750. Today, the only continental ice sheets that remain are in Greenland and Antarctica.

The ice sheet blanketing the World Heritage Site wasted away into separate glaciers. Piedmont glaciers lined a coastal plain that had been built by deposition of glacial sediments, nearly a thousand feet thick in some places, such as near the Copper River delta. Piedmont glaciers formed where the downhill flow of ice from tributary glaciers fanned out across the coastal plain and merged with other glaciers to form a lobe-shaped mass of ice.

Some piedmont glaciers still exist. Malaspina, with an area of 850 square miles (2,210 sq km), is the largest piedmont glacier in North America. Adding its 25 tributary glaciers, which extend into Kluane National Park, increases Malaspina's size to about 2,000 square miles (5,200 sq km), considerably larger than the state of Rhode Island.

The second-largest piedmont glacier is Bering, which lies east of Cordova and mostly outside the boundaries of the World Heritage Site. However, Bering Glacier begins in the Chugach Mountains at the 80-mile-long (128 km) Bagley Icefield, the largest icefield in North America. Overall, the Bering Glacier complex is the largest glacier in North America covering about 2,250 square miles (5,850 sq km), an area bigger than the state of Delaware.

As piedmont glaciers receded from the coast, **outwash plains**, made up of roughly sorted glacial material, were exposed. Glacial **till** accumulated in furrows as terminal moraines, marking temporary advances of the glacier. Recessional moraines developed where the retreat of the glacier hesitated. **Kettles** and **eskers** were left on the outwash plain as the glacier retreated.

During the Little Ice Age, ice accumulation was so heavy that it compressed underlying bedrock. When the glaciers started to retreat, the coastal areas began to rise, a process called **glacial** or **isostatic rebound**. The large outwash plain near the mouth of Glacier Bay at Bartlett Cove offers a dramatic example. Here rebound is occurring at a rate of 1.5 inches (3.8 mm)

per year, a rate that has created perceptible changes in the coastline in just a few years. It is obvious that Bartlett Cove is being left high and dry.

Some piedmont glaciers shrunk into individual **valley glaciers**. Valley glaciers plow the landscape to form U-shaped valleys, with steep, relatively smooth sides up to the **trimline**. Lateral moraines appear on each side of the glacier; medial moraines begin where the lateral moraines of two valley glaciers merge. Light and dark lines of moraine offer visible cues to the movement of giant Malaspina Glacier for airplane passengers flying between Southeast Alaska and Anchorage. Where the

In recent years, the mines and mill site at Kennecott, the abandoned company town on the slopes above Kennicott Glacier, have attracted much attention. A transcription error early in the community's history left the company and town spelled with an "e," and the river and glacier spelled with an "i," after pioneer explorer Robert Kennicott. By 1999, the National Park Service had acquired the mill buildings, shown here, and the copper mines high on the ridges overlooking the valley. (Bob Butterfield)

*Swirling clouds of silt from **loess** soil created by the grinding and scouring of Pleistocene glaciers are common in this area of Kluane's Slims River drainage known for its fierce winds. (Michael Speaks)*

open ocean. In Glacier Bay, six glaciers are now advancing, seven are stable and three are retreating. The terminus of Grand Pacific Glacier has advanced two miles (3.2 km) since 1920, moving across the border from Canada into the United States.

Some glaciers do more than advance, they surge, changing the landscape before your eyes. When a glacier surges, its movement can be 200 feet (60 m) a day or more, and most of the 204 surging glaciers in North America can be found in the World Heritage Site. Variegated Glacier, near Yakutat Bay, is the world's most studied surging glacier. It has had six surges since 1905, one every 17 years except for the last surge in 1995, which occurred after a 13-year interval. Will Harrison, a scientist with the University of Alaska Fairbanks, has been studying this glacier since 1971. "Surges occur when a glacier's internal plumbing fails," Harrison says. "The failure leads to high water pressure under the glacier, then probably to partial flotation. The result is loss of friction and then movement downhill at high speed."

Alpine glaciers, another common feature of the World Heritage Site, are the smallest glaciers but create perhaps the most scenic views. These glaciers, or cirques, cling to bowl-shaped depressions carved by ice high on the mountainside. A type of crevasse called a bergschrund separates the glacier from the mountainside. The cirque will be partially surrounded by one or more aretes, which are steep, jagged ridges. When the glacier melts away, it leaves a lush mountain meadow.

Glaciers can function as ice dams, blocking the flow of rivers or tides. Eventually, the water builds up so much pressure behind the barrier that it bursts through the ice dam, releasing an

gradient gets steep, crevasses, the equivalent of rapids in a river, break the surface with a maze of deep cracks in the ice. In some parts of the World Heritage Site, the main stem of the valley glacier has melted away, leaving a **hanging glacier** stranded well above the valley floor.

Valley glaciers that reach sea level are called tidewater glaciers. By the late 1990s, Glacier Bay had 13 tidewater glaciers, which **calve** icebergs into five of the park's 10 fiords. In addition, on Glacier Bay's outer coast, two tidewater glaciers deposit icebergs into Lituya Bay and one, LaPerouse Glacier, is the only glacier in North America that calves directly into the instant, devastating flood called a **jokulhlaup**. More than a century ago, Lowell Glacier in Kluane National Park advanced, creating a lake that was 50 miles (80 km) long and 300 feet (91 m) deep. When it burst in 1850, it generated a huge flood that swept down the Alsek River to Dry Bay, leaving scars on the landscape that can still be seen. A more recent jokulhlaup occurred when Hubbard Glacier, which was blocking Russell Fiord, burst in 1986, releasing 87,400 square yards (69,920 sq m) of water per second during its peak discharge, the largest outburst flood in recent history.

Hubbard Glacier's tendency to surge has been known for centuries and its movement has misled some early explorers. In 1700 the glacier retreated. When Alessandro Malaspina, an Italian working for Spain, entered Yakutat Bay in 1791, he had "a map showing the possible western end of the elusive 'Northwest Passage' at the head of the bay," according to U.S. Geological Survey reports. Malaspina's "observations within the bay indicate that the glacier had retreated at least 12.4 miles (20 km) since 1700 A.D., but beyond that point the bay was blocked by 'perpetual frost.' Malaspina named Disenchantment Bay for his frustrated hopes of finding a navigable passage."

Experiencing the Ice Age

Remnants of the Little Ice Age rule this landscape and the best overview of these glaciers is from an airplane. A flight from Juneau to Anchorage follows an arc that, on a clear day, provides spectacular views of the glaciers that dominate the landscape. Only from the air can we clearly see long valley glaciers radiating out, like twisting tentacles of various lengths, from massive icefields.

One of the more astonishing revelations from the air is the amount of landscape still covered by glaciers. The first mountains seen on a flight from Juneau to Anchorage are the St. Elias, with glaciers covering an area of about 4,556 square miles (11,845 sq km) just in Alaska. Next come the Wrangell Mountains with 3,205 square miles (8,333 sq km) of glaciers and finally the Chugach Mountains with 4,055 square miles (10,543 sq km) of glaciated landscape. The view gives us a glimpse of what the Ice Age must have been like.

But the experience is not complete without an up-close view of these massive ice bodies. A popular way to experience glaciers is via a

Dense patches of coastal vegetation indicate that Dundas Bay, off Icy Strait, is one of the few areas to avoid the heavy hand of ice during the most recent glaciation. (John Hyde/Wild Things)

Glacier Bay boat trip. Cruise ships and smaller excursion vessels make daily runs during the summer, covering the entire length of the 65-mile (105 km) fiord. As your boat glides up to the face of a tidewater glacier, the first thing you notice is that much of the ice has a deep blue color, particularly on overcast days. Ice that has been compacted by pressure, which is what happens within the glacier, reflects the blue wavelengths of light, hence the color.

Quietly, your ship drifts closer. You are astonished by the glacier's size, a wall of ice towers hundreds of feet above the water, dwarfing even your cruise liner. Hushed, you listen to the sounds: You hear the constant popping from melting bergy bits (small icebergs) as pockets of air trapped in the ice hundreds, maybe thousands, of years ago are suddenly released. You are thrilled when a loud cracking sound echoes across the water as a glacier begins to calve. The rifle-shot sounds are followed by a crashing boom as tons of ice fall into the water. Although countless rolls of film and videotape record the event, there is no substitute for just being there.

Now you know the feeling of the ebullient John Muir, who, witnessing a similar scene a century ago, wrote in *Travels in Alaska* (1979), "We turned and sailed away, joining the outgoing bergs, while 'Gloria in excelsis' still seemed to be sounding over all the white landscape, and our burning hearts were ready for any fate, feeling that, whatever the future might have in store, the treasures we had gained this glorious morning would enrich our lives forever."

While the glory of the geology of this World Heritage Site provides incredible scenery at a scale that far exceeds any human-built struc-

tures, its real beauty is the chance to witness the opposing forces of plate tectonics and glaciation. Here the land is ever changing. While the word "awesome" may be overused nowadays, this is one place where frequent use is appropriate. It becomes even more awesome when you piece together how geology influences the climate and how that has affected every form of life in this vast wilderness. ▲

On the Other Side of the Mountains:
Climatic Extremes and Contrasts

Climatic extremes and contrasts add another dimension to this World Heritage Site. If the criteria for World Heritage status included outstanding examples of climate, the four Alaska and Canadian parks would qualify on that criterion alone. The maritime climate of the Gulf of Alaska and its coastal fringe has some of the stormiest and wettest weather on earth. In contrast, the much drier continental climate of the Interior has produced some of the coldest winter temperatures in North America. In between lies a narrow zone of transitional climate with slightly more moderate weather. I have lived in all three climatic zones and what characterizes each to me is the kind of boots I need.

A maritime climate influences the land that lies between the Gulf of Alaska and the coastal mountains, which bar maritime weather from reaching inland areas. The narrow strip of land between Cross Sound and the Copper River lies within the northernmost part of this climatic zone, one that stretches from northern California to Kodiak Island.

Coastal weather is dominated by intense Aleutian low-pressure systems that blow in from the Pacific Ocean. These systems generate frequent rain in late summer and fall, and snow, rain or snain (a term residents of Southeast Alaska have for snow and rain) in the winter. Rubber knee-high boots are standard footwear here.

Some of the windiest and wettest fall storms come from the fading fury of typhoons that begin in the South Pacific and end up in the Gulf of Alaska. When these moisture-laden storms slam into the steep slopes of the St. Elias Mountains, they unload what may be not only the highest snowfall in the world, but the greatest amount of total precipitation as well. George Taylor, state climatologist for the Oregon Climate Center which is producing new climate maps for the entire United States says center staff have found an area of more than 500 inches (1270 cm) of precipitation in the Mount St. Elias vicinity. Until now, Mount Waialeale in Kauai, which receives about than 450 inches (1143 cm) of rainfall every year, has been considered the wettest spot on earth.

Gulf of Alaska water temperatures range from 43 to 45 degrees (6 to 7 C) in the winter and 55 to 57 degrees (13 to 14 C) in summer. This relatively slight difference moderates coastal land temperatures. Summer temperatures seldom get too warm (some would say never) and winter temperatures are mild, at least compared to readings elsewhere in Alaska.

A continental climatic zone, strongly influenced by Siberian high-pressure systems, dictates the weather for the interior of Alaska, most of the Yukon and northern British

ABOVE:
Visitors to Glacier Bay, such as this family breaking for lunch on the shores of Muir Inlet, need always be prepared for wet weather. Rain, mist and low clouds typify daily fare. (Roy Corral)

ABOVE, RIGHT:
Greg Simpson makes a water crossing of Lakina Creek in the Chitina Valley, where wintertime temperatures can reach minus 40 (minus 39.6 C). (Cross Fox Photography)

Columbia. This is the frigid north, made famous by writers Jack London and Robert Service. Service said in his *The Spell of the Yukon*:

The summer! No sweeter was ever:
The sunshiney woods all athrill:
The winter! The brightness that blinds you:
The white land locked tight as a drum.

In this land of the midnight sun, mild and often clear summer days have a special gentleness. Except for some mountain wind tunnels like the Slims River in Kluane, winds usually blow softly. The Wrangell and St. Elias mountains create a huge rain shadow for the Interior. Although parts of the continental zone receive less rainfall than some deserts, the ground is often wet, sometimes swampy, because of virtually no evaporation during the six months or more of winter and low evaporation rates during the rest of the year.

Some of the coldest temperatures in North America have been recorded just north of the Wrangell and St. Elias mountains. At Snag Creek, near Kluane National Park, the temperature dipped to 81 below (minus 63.0 C) in February 1947, the coldest recorded temperature in North America. When a Siberian high-pressure system settles in, the cold air will be perfectly still, almost frozen in place. In

January 1989, during one of these cold spells, Northway experienced the highest barometric pressure recorded in the United States. This is a climate where insulated mukluks or boots are worn nearly half the year.

Besides being bitter cold, winters are long, lasting well past the official start of spring. When Robert Service speaks of the winter brightness, he is referring to a land that is still frozen, even though it may be March or April, with brilliant sunlight reflecting off the snow. For a few weeks on either side of winter solstice on December 21, the continental side of the Wrangell and St. Elias mountains will have only about five hours per day of daylight. The sun will rise just to the left of due south and soon set not far to the right, never lifting more than a few degrees above the horizon. Though the weak sun radiates a soft, yellow glow at midday, most of its energy is filtered out by the atmosphere and carries no perceivable warmth.

The transitional climatic zone is just that. This zone lacks the drenching rainfall typical of the maritime climate and isn't quite as dry as the continental climate. It tends to have cool summers and cold winters, but not the extreme

The largest glacial complex in North America begins in the Bagley Icefield astride the Chugach Mountains and flows to the sea as Bering Glacier. Vitus Lake at the foot of the glacier contains the largest icebergs of any freshwater system on the continent. Such a massive complex is fed by the tremendous precipitation that Aleutian low-pressure systems carry to the Gulf of Alaska coast. (John Hyde/Wild Things)

The two largest rivers draining the World Heritage Site both empty into the Gulf of Alaska after working their way through or around the coastal mountain barrier. The Copper River skirts the Wrangells, powers its way through the Chugach Mountains and fans out into a delta east of Cordova. The Alsek, shown here with rafters on a sunny day, breaches the St. Elias Mountains and enters a huge outwash plain at Dry Bay in Glacier Bay National Preserve. (George Matz)

harshness of interior winters. The Chitina River valley, between the Chugach Mountains and the Wrangell Mountains, and the Glennallen area have a transitional climate that may be more continental than maritime. Most of the Tatshenshini-Alsek Wilderness Provincial Park has a transitional climate that leans more toward maritime than continental. This climate requires rubber boots and insulated boots, but occasionally rather than daily.

Alpine weather conditions are not normally considered a separate climatic zone, but because of the large expanse of alpine in this part of the world and because climate here differs from that in both the coastal and interior lowlands, some discussion seems warranted. In the Wrangell and St. Elias mountains alpine winter temperatures more closely match those of a continental climate and precipitation is usually snow. In summer, however, alpine areas of the St. Elias and Chugach mountains have a more maritime climate and do not warm as dramatically as the interior lowlands. Snow lingers longer. Consequently, the coastal mountains will have patches of snow in the summer at lower elevations than the more interiorlike Wrangell Mountains. The best footwear here is hiking boots in the summer and skis in the winter.

Examples of Contrasts

Despite the 24 million acres included in the World Heritage Site, there are only two small communities within its core, McCarthy and Yakutat, and only a handful on the fringe. Consequently, fewer weather stations are available to collect data that can be used to compare the three climatic zones. Recently, however, a number of remote weather stations have been installed that will eventually provide more comprehensive data.

Based on available weather data, Yakutat most represents the maritime climate. It has about the same temperatures as Cordova and Gustavus, but is wetter. At the other extreme is Northway, which clearly has a continental climate. In winter, Northway's temperatures are about 15 degrees (8 C) colder than Slana in the Mentasta Mountains. In the Yukon, the Alaska Highway communities of Beaver Creek, Burwash Landing and Haines Junction also experience a continental climate. In the winter, Beaver Creek is about two degrees colder than Northway, and Haines Junction to the

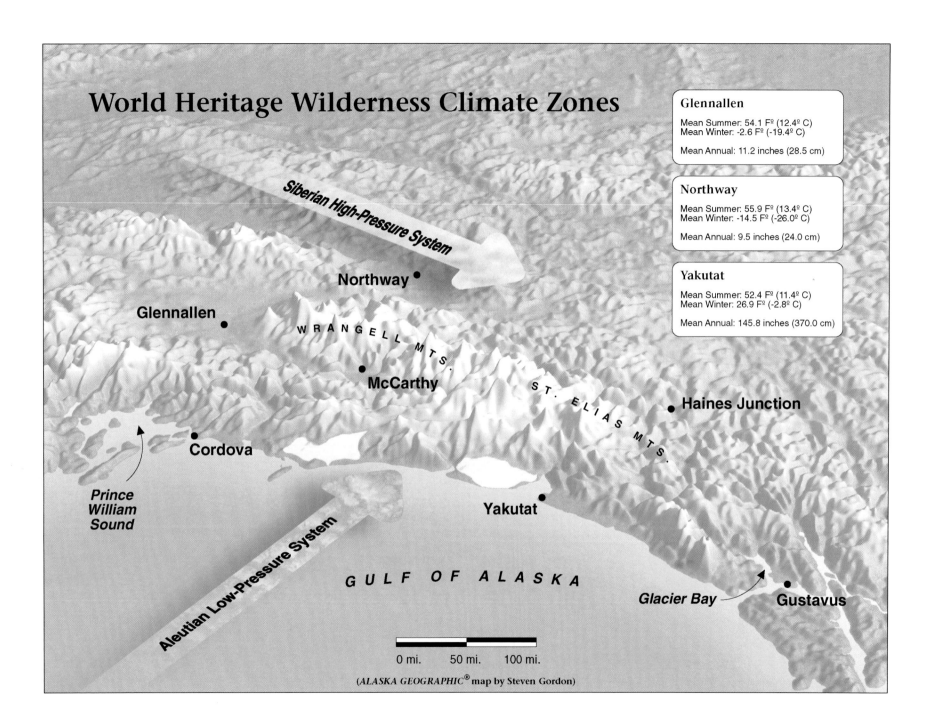

World Heritage Wilderness Climate Zones

Glennallen

Mean Summer: 54.1 F° (12.4° C)
Mean Winter: -2.6 F° (-19.4° C)

Mean Annual: 11.2 inches (28.5 cm)

Northway

Mean Summer: 55.9 F° (13.4° C)
Mean Winter: -14.5 F° (-26.0° C)

Mean Annual: 9.5 inches (24.0 cm)

Yakutat

Mean Summer: 52.4 F° (11.4° C)
Mean Winter: 26.9 F° (-2.8° C)

Mean Annual: 145.8 inches (370.0 cm)

Siberian High-Pressure System

Northway

Glennallen

W R A N G E L L   M T S.

McCarthy

S T.   E L I A S   M T S.

Haines Junction

Cordova

Prince
William
Sound

Aleutian Low-Pressure System

Yakutat

G U L F   O F   A L A S K A

Glacier Bay

Gustavus

0 mi.   50 mi.   100 mi.

(*ALASKA GEOGRAPHIC*® map by Steven Gordon)

southeast is about 10 degrees (6 C) warmer.

Glennallen, Gulkana and McCarthy are in the transitional zone, but Glennallen is most representative. The seasonal variations for Glennallen are closer to Northway's.

Mean annual precipitation for Yakutat is more than Glacier Bay or Cordova and is considerably more than Glennallen and Northway. In fact, from August through March, Yakutat usually receives more precipitation in a month than Northway, which is right on the other side of the mountains, receives all year.

Beaver Creek in the Yukon also sees more precipitation and snowfall than Northway, but the Yukon gets progressively drier toward Haines Junction. The fall storms, which deluge Yakutat with rain, are not a factor in the Interior.

Much of the precipitation that falls in this region is snow. At first glance, a climate-watcher might think that Northway, being the coldest, gets the most snow but the opposite is true. Northway averages only about 36.9 inches (93.7 cm) of snow a year. Glennallen averages 51.5 inches (130.8 cm) of snow annually and Yakutat gets dumped with an average of 193.8 inches (492.3 cm). Yakutat gets about as much snow per month from December through March as Northway gets all year.

All of this precipitation needs to go somewhere. The snow that becomes glacial ice moves downhill slowly until it reaches tidewater or turns into meltwater that trickles from a glacier. In summer, the glacial melt, the snow melt and runoff from rainfall, amount to a lot of water. Much of the water eventually reaches either the Alsek or the Copper rivers, the two major drainages for the region. The Copper ranks as the sixth largest river in the United States based on average annual discharge. These waterways nourish a varied plant community, notable for its diversity and rarity.

Native plants have successfully adapted to the limited growing conditions established by the climate. How limited this is can be seen by the **growing-degree-day** data for crops. The threshold temperature for crops typically grown in Alaska is 40 degrees (4.4 C). This doesn't include crops like corn, which has a threshold temperature of 50 degrees (9.9 C). It takes an accumulation of at least 1,500 growing-degree-days for these crops to succeed. Although Northway has the coldest winters, it has more cumulative growing-degree-days through the summer (1,770) than Glennallen (1,577) or Yakutat (1,632). But all three communities are barely above the threshold. ▲

FACING PAGE:
The fishing community of Yakutat, population 810, has a maritime climate typical of the coastal strip of the world heritage wilderness. (R.E. Johnson)

BELOW:
The interior side of the World Heritage Site receives less snow, even though it is much colder. Its annual precipitation in some areas is more akin to that of a desert, especially when compared to the abundant rain- and snowfall found on the coastal side. This view looking toward the Mentasta Mountains was taken from the Nabesna Road north of the Wrangells. (George Wuerthner)

A Crossroads for Vegetation

Like brother and sister, the physical and biological elements of the earth are distinctly different but related. Geological processes shape the landscape, the landscape strongly influences climate, and climate largely determines the type of vegetation that propagates in a particular place. In addition, geological processes create soil nutrients and drainage patterns, factors that significantly affect the diversity and abundance of plant life.

In the World Heritage Site, the connection between geology, climate and terrestrial vegetation is more pronounced than in most landscapes. Besides being a vast area that, for all practical purposes, has not been altered by human development, this isolated corner of the world has a wide array of landscapes and climate. These conditions nourish a composite of plant life. The diversity and contrasts in the vegetation types or zones that encircle the lower elevations of the four parks provide an exceptional opportunity to observe how plants adapt to their environment.

Vegetation types along the coast are much the opposite of those found in the interior lowlands. The active geology and aggressive climate of the coastal strip creates many natural disturbances, such as landslides and trees blown down by wind, that result in complex, dynamic changes in plant life.

Uplands on both sides of the mountains either have alpine tundra, represented by lichens, bearberry and heather, or are too cold for plant life.

The cool summers, mild winters and abundant precipitation that characterize the marine climate of Southeast Alaska provide ideal conditions for growth of a temperate rain forest. The rain forest here is the northern extension of the Pacific rain forest that stretches from northern California to Kodiak Island. In the World Heritage Site, this rain forest is mostly confined to the narrow coastal plain, except for the fiords of Glacier Bay and the valleys of the Alsek and Copper rivers, which slice through the coastal mountains. Here fingers of marine climate and rain forest reach farther inland.

Most of the rain forest in Glacier Bay National Park and Preserve and the sliver of coastal forest in Wrangell-St. Elias National Park and Preserve is still young and evolving. This area doesn't have much old-growth forest, but the rapid retreat of glaciers that has occurred here during the past two centuries illustrates some classic examples of primary **plant succession**. Pioneer plants, such as dryas, horsetail and fireweed, are the first to establish roots on the gravel moraines left by retreating glaciers. These plants help break down rock into soil, providing a foundation for a succession of

THE COASTAL RAIN FOREST

The canopy of the temperate rain forest that lines much of the Gulf of Alaska coast is composed of towering Sitka spruce and western hemlock, the larger trees being more than 200 feet (60 m) high and several feet in diameter. Wispy lichens hang from tree branches, and a thick tangle of berry shrubs (blueberry, huckleberry, highbush cranberry and currants) and rusty menziesia fill in the understory. Patches of devils club and skunk cabbage take over boggy areas. A profusion of herbs, ferns and moss carpet the spongy forest floor and it is often difficult to walk through this thick forest growth.

In poorly drained areas, muskeg meadows with sedges, grasses and mosses provide openings to the forest. On the edge of the forest, black cottonwood, Sitka alder, red alder and salmonberry line the beaches and riverbanks. The long coastline, with tides that range between a maximum high of 12 to 13 feet (3.6 to 3.9 m) and a minimum low of minus 2 to 3 feet (.6 to .9 m), creates extensive tidelands. Protected bays and estuaries are flush with salt-tolerant plants, such as beach rye and goose tongue.

Because of the dampness, lightning and forest fires happen rarely and an old-growth forest, with trees older than 250 years, prevails where logging or natural disturbances such as avalanches haven't occurred. Left alone, a Sitka spruce will live several hundred years. After it dies, a large tree will continue to provide habitat for numerous organisms for hundreds of years. ■

Moss-draped Sitka spruce and western hemlock mark this mature forest in the southern reaches of Glacier Bay. Since glaciers retreated from this area the earliest, vegetation here has had a chance to reach maturity. There are sections along the park's outer coast that remained ice-free during the most recent glaciation and here, too, a climax forest has developed. (George Matz)

plant communities, eventually culminating in an old-growth forest.

On the continental side of the mountains, the extreme difference between summer and winter temperatures, the lower precipitation and the shorter growing season limit the species of plants that can survive. The cold soil, often laced with permafrost just inches below the surface, also curtails plant growth. These conditions favor the boreal forest biome that encircles the earth at northern latitudes.

This stretch of boreal forest includes five general types of vegetation, the most extensive of which are the closed spruce-hardwood forest and the open, low-growing spruce forest. In addition, smaller areas, mostly north of the Wrangell Mountains, support predominately shrub thickets, moist tundra and treeless bogs.

Climatic conditions change with elevation and so does vegetation. Higher elevations equate to higher latitudes, which tend to be colder and have a shorter growing season. Approaching tree line, trees become shorter, more gnarled and spaced farther apart. In coastal areas, herbs such as false hellebore and deer cabbage are more evident nearer tree line. Thick patches of alder shrubs and subalpine meadows, with a lush growth of flowering herbs, fill a niche where trees falter. Trees are kept from germinating where a deep snowpack lingers late into the growing season or occasional avalanches wipe out anything standing. In the Interior, the boreal forest gives way at timber line to alders, willows and bluejoint grass.

Throughout North America, tree line tends to occur where the mean July temperature doesn't exceed 50 degrees (10 C), though this is subject to microclimatic factors, such as

shade, wind or the presence of glaciers. Tree line can be anywhere between sea level near tidewater glaciers to about 2,500 feet (800 m) in Glacier Bay and 3,500 to 4,000 feet (1,000 to 1,200 m) in Kluane. It may appear to be a contradiction that Kluane, with a colder climate, has a higher tree line, but its warmer summers and lighter snowpack allow trees to reach higher elevations.

Above the shrubs and subalpine meadows lies the alpine zone where herbs thrive, such as mountain harebell and glaucous gentian. A variety of mosses and lichens cover the thin, rocky soil. Mountain-heath predominates on coastal alpine slopes; dwarf birch and various berry shrubs are common on interior slopes.

Substantial private land exists within the Wrangell-St. Elias National Park portion of the World Heritage Site. Some private owners, including Alaska Native corporations, have clearcut their land, leaving broad scars on the forested hillsides. (George Wuerthner)

THE INTERIOR BOREAL FOREST

The closed spruce-hardwood forest that grows on well-drained hillsides and river valleys, such as in the Chitina River valley, is the archetype of the boreal forest. Its closed canopy (looking up, you see leaves, not sky), composed mostly of a mosaic of spruce, hardwoods and mixed stands, represents different stages in the forest succession process. Hardwood species found here include paper birch and balsam poplar, with quaking aspen more frequent on well-drained sites. Black spruce will occur in poorly drained areas.

An open spruce forest with willow (yellow) and dwarf birch (red) characterizes much of Kluane's vegetation. (George Matz)

Alders and willows are common at the forest edge but usually as shrubs less than 10 feet (3 m) high rather than as trees. The understory often has a variety of berry shrubs, particularly blueberry and prickly rose. In areas where the forest floor is not completely shaded, fireweed, bluejoint grass and horsetails grow. The understory tends to be fairly open and not difficult to walk through.

On the other hand, the open, low-growing spruce forest occupies north-facing slopes and poorly drained areas like much of the forest-and-bog country around Glennallen. Black spruce, its growth usually stunted by cold, wet soil that often has permafrost, dominates this habitat. The open canopy admits light, which favors shrub growth, and patches of alders, willows and berry shrubs, particularly lowbush cranberry, are scattered throughout the woods. This type of forest, and to a lesser degree the white spruce-birch forest, is frequently disturbed by fire, often caused by lightning. As a result, the forest seldom reaches old-growth status.

In Kluane, the white spruce, quaking aspen and balsam poplar forest is referred to as a montane forest. Interspersed throughout this habitat are dry, steppelike, grassy meadows with sage, juniper and soapberry. These meadows are reminiscent of Beringia.

The shrub thickets found in Kluane are dense patches of mostly alder, willow and resin birch, less than 10 feet (3 m) high, that are typically found between tree line and alpine areas or in wetter soils. Moist tundra meadows exist in flat, poorly drained areas, frequently marked by cottongrass, and alders, dwarf birch or other shrubs. Treeless bogs, characterized by grasses, sedges and mosses, particularly sphagnum moss, form in areas with fine clay soils that are poorly drained and too moist for trees. Commonly called muskeg, this habitat requires hikers who have to cross it to adopt a stance akin to stepping across a field of tires. ■

Farther up the slope, alpine plants either give way to bare rock or abruptly end at permanent ice and snow. But some algae actually thrives on ice and snow, such as red algae, which often appears as a pink blush on summer snow patches.

The landscape of the Wrangell and St. Elias mountains is woven with tumbling streams and rushing rivers, providing habitat for aquatic plants. However, many of the streams are too steep to have much vegetation other than algae clinging to rocks. Virtually all of the rivers are laden with glacial silt, blocking much of the sunlight that aquatic plants need for photosynthesis. But a scattering of small lakes in relatively flat areas, muskeg ponds or beaver ponds provide warmer, clearer water that is more conducive to aquatic plant growth.

Glacier Bay

All four parks have receding glaciers and excellent examples of plant succession. But Glacier Bay National Park and Preserve, with tidewater glaciers that have retreated many miles in just a few decades, best illustrates the stages during which a landscape matures from pioneer species to old-growth forest. Glacier Bay has been recognized as a classic example of plant succession ever since John Muir first visited in 1879. Less recognized are the examples of seaweed, or marine algae, succession visible in its fiords. As glaciers retreat, seaweed quickly becomes established in new habitat, a process most easily observed in intertidal areas.

I have kayaked most of Glacier Bay and I think the best way to witness the progressive stages of plant succession, and to experience the sense of discovery that Muir must have

felt, is to explore the bay in a sea kayak. Air and boat services can drop you and a kayak off near the face of a glacier, where you can observe ecological succession from its stark beginnings. But it is more dramatic, and more like Muir's approach, to begin with the familiar, well-established forest and intertidal life in Bartlett Cove at the entrance to Glacier Bay, and head up-bay. The kayak becomes a time capsule, taking paddlers back in time, geologically and biologically, with each stroke. The closeness of the kayak to the shore and intertidal zone, and the ease of going ashore, provides a more intimate experience than a ride down the middle of the bay in a cruise ship.

Off-duty park ranger Adrianna Cahill explores a pond in the Alder Creek watershed south of Bartlett Cove. The pond is surrounded by vegetation typical of a mature forest. (Matthew Cahill)

Bartlett Cove was near the face of a glacier more than 200 years ago when glacial retreat began. In fact, when British explorer Capt. James Cook sailed by in 1778, there was no bay, only a towering wall of ice. Consequently, the rebirth of the Sitka spruce/western hemlock forest here has been underway longer than elsewhere within the bay and approaches old-growth status. On some of the park's outer Pacific coast and in places such as Dundas Bay, long-established old-growth forest thrives in areas spared glaciation during the Little Ice Age. Shore pine, a stunted version of lodgepole pine, is recolonizing muskeg areas near Bartlett Cove where blueberry shrubs, flowery herbs and thick mosses and ferns mark the understory. Chest-high skunk cabbage and thorny devils club create nearly impenetrable patches of vegetation in places where the thin soil is saturated with water. Several short trails give hikers the sense of an older forest with streams of filtered sunlight, songs of thrushes and sparrows, and a pervading dampness.

A kayak trip should begin with an overnight stay at the Bartlett Cove campground that is next to a coastal rain forest beach, typical of Southeast Alaska. Alders grow above the high tide mark, creating a buffer of shrubs between the forest and the beach rye that dominates the higher intertidal area. Salmonberry and wild strawberry sprout where gaps in the alders allow sunlight to penetrate. Colorful flowering plants, such as chocolate lily, lupine, paintbrush and cow parsnip bloom profusely in the upper intertidal area in June and early July. Lower on the beach appear beach pea, beach greens and other plants more tolerant of exposure to salt water. Goose tongue and silverweed occupy the mean high tide zone.

Rockweed, or *Fucus*, covers the rocks and gravel in the intertidal area.

Climbing into a kayak at Bartlett Cove and paddling up the bay, you soon come to the Beardslees, a cluster of low, forested islands that are uplifting as much as 1.5 inches (3.8 cm) a year due to glacial rebound. The forest edge, advancing toward the water, and the widening of the intertidal area testifies to the uplift.

Mature vegetation, **successional vegetation** and rock or ice each make up about one-third of the Glacier Bay landscape. Continuing up the bay, you will notice the Sitka spruce becoming progressively shorter. Eventually the spruce forest shifts to one mixed with hardwoods, predominately cottonwood. Willow is fairly common, unusual for Southeast, creating good habitat for moose. About halfway up the bay, the forest becomes mostly young cottonwood mixed with alders and willows. Rockweed, also just getting established, sparsely covers the intertidal area.

As you approach the tidewater glaciers, the forest dwindles to alder and willow shrubs with a scattering of cottonwoods. Pads of dryas hold down the silt and begin soil development by adding the organic matter and nitrogen taken from the atmosphere that other plants will need. In some places, large tree trunks and stumps protrude from the mud. This wood isn't a product of the present-day forest; these trees, or "fossil wood" in Muir's terms, were buried by the advance of glaciers about 5,000 years ago, and kept in a deep freeze until uncovered by recent glacial retreat. Holding a piece of interglacial wood impregnated with silt but not fossilized is like momentarily stepping into the past.

Farther up the bay, the rock-and-gravel landscape becomes nearly void of plant life. An occasional pad of dryas appears to be catching hold and a clump of dwarf fireweed clings to a ledge, but this is it. Here is the beginning of a forest. Someday this barren landscape may be covered with huge trees, like at Bartlett Cove. After paddling from forest to glaciers, I could now visualize the progression by which that may happen. I could see the land as it was, as it is, and as it will be.

Tatshenshini-Alsek

Tatshenshini-Alsek Wilderness Provincial Park is flanked by high mountains on both its

FACING PAGE:
This marsh on Kidney Island, one of the Beardslee group in Glacier Bay, was once a saltwater channel. As glacial or isostatic rebound causes the land to rise, the marsh will dry and eventually be covered by trees. (Scott Croll)

BELOW:
The common red paintbrush can be found in both seashore and subalpine meadows of Glacier Bay. (Scott Croll)

coastal and interior sides, which block maritime low-pressure storms and continental high-pressure cold. The result is a more moderate transitional climate with vegetation representative of both boreal forest and rain forest.

A white/black spruce forest covers about 12 percent of the park. The subalpine spruce-willow-birch forest fills in about 19 percent. In the Alsek River valley, this latter zone extends from the valley bottom to the high country and includes aspen as well as some lodgepole pine. Alpine tundra begins at elevations above 3,000

feet (1,000 m), or less near glaciers. The alpine zone covers about 68 percent of the park, illustrating its mountainous character. Plants typical of the alpine, where it isn't just rock or ice, are mountain heather, mountain avens and crowberry.

In the eastern end of the park, some drainages flow into Lynn Canal and are more like a coastal rain forest. Mountain hemlock grow near tree line and coastal western hemlock at lower elevations. Sitka spruce and subalpine fir are common here, especially bordering creeks.

The presence of subalpine fir, and lodgepole pine in drier areas, represents the northern extension of a Rocky-Mountain-type of forest. This extra dose of biodiversity gives the Tatshenshini-Alsek a flavor that the other parks lack.

The best way to experience the diverse flora of this magnificent park is to raft either the Tatshenshini or Alsek rivers. Either trip crosses the heart of the park, providing not only a good profile of its plant life, but also outstanding scenery and whitewater thrills. I floated the "Tat" in August 1997 and agree with those who advocated establishing the park; it does offer an exceptional combination of untarnished natural history, wilderness beauty and, at times, adrenaline-pumping excitement.

My Tatshenshini trip began at Dalton Post off the Haines Highway in the foothills of the Coast Mountains. From here the river winds for a few miles through the Yukon and then into British Columbia. The upper Tat flows through a valley of boreal white/black spruce forest in the lowlands, a spruce-willow-birch forest along mountain slopes and alpine tundra at higher elevations. Black cottonwoods dominate the floodplain with Sitka alder making up most of the understory. As you float down the river, the cottonwoods get smaller and then give way, as you enter the core of the St. Elias Mountains, to just tundra with patches of alder on the outwash plains of numerous glaciers.

The Tat is a tributary of the Alsek River, joining it just before the British Columbia-Alaska border. After these big rivers merge, the even wider Alsek cuts through the St. Elias Mountains, giving the impression that you are floating through a canyon with alder shrubs lining the riverbank. As you pass through this spectacular scenery, small cottonwoods reappear, becoming larger as the Alsek nears Dry Bay in Glacier Bay National Preserve. Where the river spills out onto the vast Dry Bay outwash plain, a major landscape feature on this section of the coast, the cottonwoods blend into the young Sitka spruce/western hemlock rain forest. If you find the right channel for your raft, you come across a small landing strip for chartered planes, 140 river miles from where the trip started. There are no options for a shorter trip, but you're in for a longer trip if you miss the channel.

Floating the Tat is much different than kayaking Glacier Bay when it comes to observing plant life. Considering the early age of the Tat-Alsek forest, its transitional setting between a boreal forest and coastal rain forest, its close proximity to a Rocky-Mountain-type forest and the uncertainties of global warming, paddlers are encouraged to speculate about which type of forest will prevail a century from now. The options here seem to be more complex than at Glacier Bay where a coastal rain forest is steadily advancing up the bay as climate warms.

Oysterleaf clings to a rocky shore near Margerie Glacier, another example of plant succession, which plays a big role in Glacier Bay's story. (Matthew Cahill)

Kluane

The Icefield Range of the St. Elias Mountains takes up most of Kluane National Park and, as the name implies, is virtually all rock and ice with no vegetation. About 82 percent of the park is unvegetated. However, lower elevations of the Kluane Range — the mountains visible from the Alaska Highway — support a mix of forest, meadow and alpine tundra. Kluane is renowned as a botanical crossroads and its diverse habitats support about 100 plant communities composed of 871 species. Among these species are ones more typical of the northern prairies, the Rocky Mountains and even the steppes of Siberia.

Although Kluane has more exotic species than the other parks, it also lacks some species typical of the boreal forest. Most interesting is

that there is no black spruce or paper birch within Kluane's boundaries. However, these trees, which prefer wetter soil than Kluane offers, are common nearby. Extensive open forests of black spruce carpet boggy, lower elevations associated with the Shakwak Trench that parallels the northern boundary of the park, and birch are found in the subalpine zone of Tatshenshini-Alsek park.

A good profile of Kluane flora can be seen by hiking one of several trails that begin at either the Alaska or Haines highways. The Slims River and Alsek River trails off the Alaska Highway are drier, because they fall more directly in the St. Elias rain shadow, and have more of a steppelike Beringia appearance.

In 1998 I hiked the 17-mile (29 km) Alsek River Valley Trail, which follows an old mining road paralleling the Dezadeash River from where it begins to cut through the Kluane Range to where it merges with the Alsek River. This trail traverses a spruce-hardwood forest zone that covers only 7 percent of Kluane's land surface but nearly half of its vegetated area. Forested segments of the trail have either a closed canopy of white spruce or an open canopy with spruce and stunted hardwoods, such as balsam poplar and quaking aspen, as well as willow and alder shrubs. Typical herbaceous plants include Jacob's ladder and Siberian aster. Above the forest zone lies a subalpine zone with tall shrubs, typically alders and willows. Above this is alpine tundra with stunted shrubs such as blueberry and crowberry, small herbaceous plants like gentian and mountain avens, mosses and lichens.

Near the beginning of the trail are stands of dead mature white spruce that have been killed by the same species of bark beetle that has in-

fested the Copper River basin and the Kenai Peninsula in Southcentral Alaska. Although park naturalists recognize this beetle as indigenous to the area, they believe that more extensive infestations can be traced to the building of the Alaska Highway more than 50 years ago. In clearing the highway, piles of spruce trees were stacked up, creating abundant breeding areas for the beetle. Since then, higher levels of infestation have continued.

Hiking along the trail, I noted extensive meadows with bluegrass, wheatgrass, sage and juniper, that seem atypical of a boreal forest. Some of the sages are Eurasian species rare in North America. Other species include

Dark purple monkshood and lavender Jacob's ladder brighten a moist field in the Wrangells. (Bill Sherwonit)

soapberry, prickly rose, fireweed and plants common to the boreal forest. The desertlike vegetation combined with the loose texture of the loess soil gave me the feeling that I had entered a time warp and was now back tens of thousands of years, experiencing what Beringia was like during the Ice Age. Sitting on a rock, I surveyed the landscape and envisioned a cold, dry, grassy plain with bison and woolly mammoths wandering about. A chill wind blowing up the river valley added to the effect.

After a couple of miles, I came to an area where, not long ago, the trail was at the bottom of Lake Alsek. This lake forms whenever Lowell Glacier, about 50 miles (75 km) downstream, surges and blocks the Alsek River, an event that has happened four times in the past few hundred years. Eventually the ice dam breaks and the lake drains in one huge flood, or jokulhlaup, the most recent being about 1850. Consequently, lower parts of the trail have only recently become dry land and have revegetated.

After finishing the hike, I once again had the feeling that I had tumbled into the past, that the landscape across which I had traveled was tethered to the Beringia of Pleistocene times. Observing the plant life was the key to envisioning this ancient world.

Wrangell St. Elias

Wrangell-St. Elias National Park and Preserve has the greatest variety of landscapes, climates and plant species of the four parks. Recent field studies by botanists have found 884 vascular species in the park, of which 215 species are additions to the park's list of flora and 10 are additions to the state's list. This list of species represents 90 percent of Alaska's flora. The field work discovered 80 rare plants and 24 that are endemic to Alaska or the Yukon. The sedge, grass, sunflower and mustard families have the largest number of species. In addition, more than 100 species of mosses and lichens were found.

Most of the landscape consists of either alpine tundra or glaciers and icefields. A spruce-hardwood forest and other ecosystems, such as muskeg, occupy all but 10 percent of the remaining land surface. The coastal rain forest of Sitka spruce and western hemlock, and wave-stirred beaches, account for the remaining surface area.

Above tree line, slopes not covered with glaciers or icefields have thin, rocky soil with little vegetation. The vegetation that does exist is dominated by mat-forming dwarf shrubs such as mountain avens, low-bush cranberry, bog blueberry, crowberry and willow. Lichens, which look like an aerial view of a miniature forest from the eye level of a standing human, can be just as extensive as shrubs. Rocky, south-facing slopes may have sage, with its distinct aroma prized by Native people who burned it as incense. Typical herbaceous plants include sedges, anemone and some species of saxifrage.

A rolling boreal forest covers the gradual slope that comes off Mount Drum (12,010 ft./ 3,643 m) on the western side of the park. This forest also crawls up the valleys of the rivers that flow from the center of the mountains. I think the best profile of the park's forest can be had by driving from Glennallen to McCarthy and then hiking some of the trails. This route parallels the Copper River for 67 highway miles (107 km) from Glennallen to the end of the Edgerton Highway in Chitina, and then continues along the rough, gravel McCarthy

Road for another 59 miles (94 km), following the Chitina River most of the way. The McCarthy Road is the longest of the two roads that penetrate the park — the Nabesna Road branches off the Tok Cutoff and heads southeast to the Nabesna Mine — and it winds through the longest stretch of forest within the park.

An open black spruce forest mixed with stands of paper birch and quaking aspen carpets the 1,500-to-2,000-foot (460 to 600 m) plateau in the Glennallen area. Alder and numerous species of willows are common, but grow only as shrubs. Other shrubs with delectable fruits, such as blueberry, low-bush cranberry and prickly rose, as well as Labrador tea, cover much of the understory. Lupine, northern yarrow,

FACING PAGE:
The Dixie Pass area above Strelna in the Wrangells offers a prime example of alpine vegetation. Moss and lichens hold the thin soil, but even they must give way to ice and snow in the extreme elevations of much of this wilderness. (Vince Franke)

BELOW:
Kristin Hostetter and Annie Getchell hike a trail lined with willows and grasses near Grizzly Lake in the Wrangells in fall. Trails above the lake make easy hiking, allowing visitors to enjoy the vista and watch for Dall sheep. (Kate Salisbury)

triangular-leaved fleabane and Ross avens flourish here, sprouting from ground covered with a cushion of sphagnum moss.

Last summer on a drive south from Glennallen, my wife and I followed the Richardson Highway and noticed a closed canopy white spruce-hardwood forest. Most of the birch had been replaced by aspen, which better tolerate the drier soil. We turned onto the Edgerton Highway, where the road passed a scattering of small farms and settlements near Kenny Lake and then gradually climbed, offering good views of the forest and mountains.

Approaching Chitina, we saw extensive areas of dead white spruce killed by the spruce bark beetle. Although the beetle is indigenous to this forest and outbreaks have occurred previously, the one still underway appears to be more widespread and persistent. How to handle the epidemic has sparked controversy in Southcentral Alaska, where populated regions fear wildfires in beetle-killed forests. Most agree that control of the beetle on a landscape-scale is not feasible, but some want to log the trees to capture economic gain before decay sets in. Others want to minimize the ecological impact that large-scale salvage logging would cause.

Just north of Chitina and along the first few miles of the McCarthy Road, much of the land is owned by the Ahtna Native Corp., which opted to clearcut large swaths of forest. The National Park Service, whose land appeared ahead as we continued toward McCarthy, chose to treat the beetle infestation as a natural event and allow the forest to regenerate on its own. The clearcuts are a lot more obvious than the stands of dead spruce that soon turn gray and blend in with the younger trees that remain.

The road past Chitina parallels a wide floodplain with numerous small, grass-lined lakes and a dense spruce, aspen and balsam poplar forest, interspersed with treeless bogs and shrub thickets. Approaching McCarthy, the spruce give way to aspen, poplar, alders and willows, although the trees are somewhat stunted since the elevation is closer to tree line. In the understory, soapberry, whose bitter-tasting berry attracts bears, has replaced blueberries and lowbush cranberries.

After reaching McCarthy, my wife and I hiked along McCarthy Creek to observe the forest understory. We found a mosaic of prickly rose, highbush cranberry, Siberian aster, Eskimo potato and dwarf dogwood. The gravel bars along the creek had patches of pioneer species such as dryas and fireweed. It was a pleasant hike but one that would be spectacular in early September when golden-colored leaves shimmered on the balsam poplar and aspen that comprise most of the canopy.

The four world heritage parks share some of the same plant life, but each has distinct species due to differences in landscape and climate. This composite of plant life, which has received far less study than in most national parks, offers opportunities for new discoveries by professional botanists and new insight by those who are merely fascinated with the complexities and marvels of ecosystems. The four parks truly provide outstanding examples of plant communities, one of the criteria for Natural World Heritage Sites. ▲

Wood Frogs to Whales:
World Heritage Wildlife

Whoosh! A behemoth propels itself from the water, climbs until tons of bulk are silhouetted against glacier or sky, then crashes back into the sea, spray flying in all directions. Whether watching a humpback whale breach in Glacier Bay, a brown bear amble across a glacial outwash plain in the Alsek River valley, a herd of Dall sheep cling to a mountain cliff in Kluane, or a bald eagle perch in a tall spruce above the Copper River, the setting, as much as the sighting, is what makes this world heritage wilderness a memorable place for wildlife observation.

The geology, climate and flora of the four parks come together to create some of the best and most varied habitat that exists for northern ecosystems. While this wild country is not densely populated with animals, it does exemplify the north. Many of the larger mammals, such as brown bear and caribou, require vast areas of habitat. The 24 million acres included in the World Heritage Site provide the expansive range these species need and offer an opportunity to witness wildlife in ecosystems governed by nature rather than managed for human consumption. That is not to say that there is no evidence of human presence now or even during the last several thousand years, but that presence has been minimal.

The marine, coastal rain forest, boreal forest and alpine tundra ecosystems support a number of mammal, bird, fish and invertebrate species. This diversity, however, does not extend to reptiles and amphibians. There are no reptiles in any of the four parks and only two species of amphibians: the wood frog and the boreal or western toad. The wood frog, fairly common in moist woodlands throughout Alaska and the Yukon, has the unusual ability to freeze solid during the winter without rupturing its cells, and then to fully recover when thawed. The secretive boreal or western toad occurs mostly in forested areas near water. The three species of salamanders that occur in Alaska are doubtful residents of any of the four parks.

Ecosystems

A biologically rich marine ecosystem borders coastal areas of this World Heritage Site and penetrates inland via numerous fiords that often teem with bleating seals, squawking birds and other noisy wildlife. I find these raucous environs thrilling. Glacier Bay is exceptional in that it is a microcosm of the North Pacific, supporting a full range of marine mammals, seabirds, waterfowl, anadromous fish and bottomfish, mollusks and other invertebrates.

The Gulf of Alaska adds to the overall diversity of the region. Here upwelling of nutrients creates an abundance of phytoplankton, the

vital first link in the ocean's food chain. The phytoplankton are eaten by zooplankton, which, in turn, attract seabirds and marine mammals that migrate along the Pacific Coast to the Gulf for a summer-long feast. In addition to the humpback, minke and killer whales often seen within Glacier Bay, fin whales congregate near Cross Sound, gray whales and northern fur seals pass on their way to and from the Bering Sea, and an occasional northern elephant seal probes this far north. Large colonies of seabirds nest on land, often on rocky islands, but spend winter at sea.

The rain forest is home to many species of animals that depend on old-growth forest. When alive, a large Sitka spruce or western hemlock provides shelter from harsh weather, particularly deep snow that would otherwise exhaust some foraging animals such as Sitka black-tailed deer. After it dies, the tree's usefulness continues. A log, rotting on the ground, supports a miniature ecosystem of small animals ranging from weasels that den in the log, to numerous beetles, called decomposers, that feed on dead wood. A fallen tree lying in a stream will back up water into a pool, providing essential habitat for salmon and other fish.

The only large land mammal exclusive to the region's coastal rain forest is the Sitka black-tailed deer. Birds that are fairly common year-round residents of this environment, but not other ecosystems, include the great blue heron, the Vancouver Canada goose, blue grouse, red-breasted sapsucker, northwestern crow, Steller's jay, winter wren and chestnut-backed chickadee. In addition, the coastal rain forest shelters a variety of nesting neotropical songbirds including the barn swallow, Pacific-slope flycatcher and western tanager.

The cutthroat trout, a popular sport fish, inhabits freshwater lakes in the rain forest, but not in the boreal forest. Pacific herring spawn in estuaries and anadromous eulachon, or hooligan, rely on coastal habitat for food and shelter. Each species is a vital food source for other fish, as well as many birds and mammals. One of the most amazing spectacles I have ever witnessed was herring spawning in a small cove near Lynn Canal. White gel, sprinkled with small, dark eggs coated the entire intertidal area.

The boreal forest is nearly as productive as any other ecosystem during the short, intense summer. Long hours of sunlight and warm, but not scorching, temperatures prove ideal for plants that germinate quickly. Winter is just the opposite. There is virtually no plant growth and animals must live off the summer surplus, seeds and twigs, or prey on animals that do. The contrast between the seasons requires animals to adapt. For example, moose browse on lush vegetation during the summer. As winter approaches, their body chemistry changes to produce enzymes needed to digest the birch and willow twigs that will sustain them during the next few months. Without this shift in body chemistry, moose would not survive the long winter.

The boreal forest, unlike the coastal rain forest, supports such mammals as barren-ground and woodland caribou, bison, coyote and red fox. Spruce grouse, northern hawk owl, northern flicker, Hammond's flycatcher, gray jay, boreal chickadee and common redpoll typify species exclusive to this ecosystem. Most of the other songbirds that nest here can also be found in the rain forest. Grayling and northern pike occur in boreal forest lakes but not in coastal forest waters.

The alpine tundra also holds a few surprises. Here some shorebirds, such as American golden plovers and surfbirds, nest far from any shore. Another surprising alpine nester is the horned lark, a bird common to short-grass prairies of the Midwest. The marbled murrelet, a seabird whose nests have only recently been discovered in old-growth hemlock, has also been observed tending eggs and chicks in alpine tundra, which is also home to all three species of ptarmigan, willow, white-tailed and rock. During the

breeding season, the alpine tundra attracts species from large predators to tiny songbirds: golden eagles, gyrfalcons, northern harriers, Townsend's solitaires, American pipits, Lapland longspurs and rosy finches patrol the skies.

Dall sheep and mountain goats live almost exclusively in the alpine zone where they are joined occasionally by a member of the weasel family with a ferocious reputation, the wolverine. Although the elusive wolverine is difficult to spot, it is most often seen traveling the uplands. The tiny collared pika lives in rock piles and voles burrow through the grasses in this same habitat. Pika, members of the rabbit family, store enough food in summer to remain active all winter beneath snow-covered boulders. The fat, hoary marmot and its slimmer relative, the arctic ground squirrel, are common and are often heard before seen as their whistles rebound across mountain slopes.

Above the alpine tundra, glaciers and icefields create another ecosystem. Despite the foreboding environment, animals have adapted to these harsh conditions. The most famous is a tiny animal with an almost-mystical reputation, the iceworm, a small segmented worm that actually lives in the ice and feeds on detritus such as leaves and pollen blown onto the glacier. This organism is so adjusted to freezing temperatures that it will shrivel and die from the heat of a person's hand. The abundance of iceworms on some glaciers attracts alpine birds such as the rosy finch that apparently never learned how to search for worms in a lawn. Some species just like to do things the hard way.

A number of mammals are habitat generalists and can be found in two or more ecosystems. Brown bears and wolves roam the coastal forest, boreal forest and alpine tundra. Black bears, lynx, pine marten, weasels, snowshoe hare, red squirrels, flying squirrels, porcupines, voles, mice, shrews and the little brown bat inhabit both the rain forest and the boreal forest. Beaver, and to a lesser degree muskrats, are common in freshwater ponds and streams of both forests except on some islands. Mink and river otters are found in both fresh- and salt water.

Most birds restrict themselves to a fairly specific type of habitat. The Townsend's warbler, for instance, nests only in mature spruce forests, even trees that have been killed by bark beetles. But some birds are habitat generalists also. The American robin, the icon of suburbia, is also at home on alpine tundra. One of the most successful generalists is the raven, which inhabits just about every western ecosystem from the cold arctic tundra to the hot deserts of the southwest.

Migration

Migration is essential to wildlife that inhabit this part of the world. Moose and Sitka black-tailed deer, after foraging among subalpine shrubs and alpine meadows most of the summer, move to lower elevations in the fall where tall trees shelter them from deep snow. Mountain goats migrate from exposed cliffs to mountain hemlock stands near the tree limit. Some marine mammals head for much warmer waters; humpback whales overwinter in Hawaii. Many brown bears, however, move up to alpine areas as winter approaches to be assured of dens with snow deep enough to insulate them from the cold. Smaller mammals that cannot travel far, such as ground squirrels and marmots, simply hibernate for several months. Both species have the ability to lower

their body temperature to near freezing to minimize calorie intake.

The number of bird species resident to northern ecosystems is a fraction of those that migrate through or nest here. But even resident birds migrate short distances; for instance, ptarmigan move from alpine tundra to sub-alpine shrubs as winter sets in. Songbirds that are year-round residents, such as black-capped, boreal and chestnut-backed chickadees that survive the winter by eating seeds, fly in small flocks between seed-bearing stands of spruce, birch and alder. Winter residents have adapted to fewer hours of daylight. Redpolls store seeds gathered during the day in a special organ

FACING PAGE:
Glacier bears, a rare bluish-gray color phase of the black bear, are found only in the Yakutat area. (John Hyde/Wild Things)

ABOVE:
Hoary marmots, shown here, arctic ground squirrels, pikas and voles enliven the highlands. Whistles of marmots can often be heard echoing along the slopes well before the animals are spotted. (Corinne Smith)

where they become a midnight snack, giving the redpolls sufficient energy to stay warm till daylight when they can feed again.

Some birds tend to be year-round residents but are absent for weeks or months during the winter while seeking new sources of food. Bohemian waxwings gather in big flocks during the winter and feed on berries, such as mountain ash and highbush cranberry, then move on when the food is exhausted. Bald eagles thrive on spawned out salmon and know where to find late runs during early winter

Of the three species of ptarmigan found here, willow, rock and white-tailed, the latter usually prefers the highest habitat. White-tailed ptarmigan can be distinguished from the other species by their tail, which remains white year-round. (Chlaus Lotscher)

when food is becoming scarce. The Alaska Chilkat Bald Eagle Preserve near Glacier Bay witnesses the world's largest gathering of eagles, usually around 3,000, in early winter when a late run of chum salmon spawn in the Chilkat River. One early winter day I saw in one view hundreds of bald eagles roosting in the cottonwoods that line the river.

One of the world's greatest concentrations of shorebirds occurs at the Copper River delta, the largest contiguous wetlands on North America's Pacific Coast. The delta lies off the World Heritage Site's western border and has been designated a Western Hemisphere Shorebird Reserve Network, which has a purpose similar to that of the World Heritage Site. In spring, as many as 14 million shorebirds, including nearly 100 percent of the West Coast population of western sandpipers and dunlin, stop here to rest and feed before continuing to their nesting grounds on the tundra. I have seen flocks of shorebirds here so numerous that they resembled a tornado as they swirled above the tidal flats.

Many species of songbirds migrate to northern ecosystems to feast on the bountiful insects, berries and other food available during the brief, but productive summer. Abundant food not only fuels migrations but assures better success in raising young. Northern ecosystems, being free of snakes, also provide safer conditions for birds that nest on or near the ground. Families of migrant songbirds common to all the parks include flycatchers, swallows, thrushes, kinglets, warblers and sparrows.

Perhaps the animals with the most intriguing migration patterns are the five species of anadromous salmon — king/chinook, silver/

WETLANDS

A summertime drive along the Alaska Highway between the Canadian border and Tetlin offers vistas to the southwest of wetlands wearing a coat of many greens, fringed by the Nutzotin Mountains, and framed by the snow-capped bulk of the Wrangells. Although mountains are not usually thought of as ideal waterfowl habitat, these mountains are flanked by wetlands of international repute for between the heights and the highway lies Tetlin National Wildlife Refuge. Amphibians and fish use these wetlands, but it's much easier to see why green-winged teal, mallards, pintails, northern shovelers or American wigeon might take to Tetlin. Lakes, ponds and snaking waterways fill the lowlands. Here lesser and greater scaup, distinguished primarily by subtle differences in the color and shape of the head, and common and Barrow's goldeneye, each sporting a different-shaped white patch on the head, spend the summer. Stopping at one of the highway pullouts and scanning the ponds could bring to view a small duck with an oversized head, the bufflehead. The male of this species has brilliant white plumage on a quarter of its head and much of its body, visible for some distance.

Other waterfowl species can be found here and in wetlands throughout the World Heritage Site. Look for white-winged and surf scoters, Canada geese and common and red-breasted mergansers. Enjoy the unmistakable cackle and head-bobbing antics of mating red-necked and horned grebes, and pause to listen to the haunting calls of common, Pacific and red-throated loons, which say wilderness if nothing else does.

Not only do wetlands serve waterfowl, they also shelter smaller denizens of the wildlife kingdom. This boreal toad has found its niche in Glacier Bay National Park. (Scott Croll)

coho, red/sockeye, chum/dog, pink/humpback — that spawn in all the parks except Kluane. Salmon aren't the only fish that are anadromous, ascending freshwater rivers from the sea to breed. Rainbow trout called steelhead, highly prized by sportfishermen, are also anadromous, but unlike salmon, do not always die after spawning. Dolly Varden are usually a freshwater fish but can also be anadromous. Even strictly freshwater fish such as the arctic grayling migrate from shallow waters used for summer feeding to deeper waters that don't freeze solid to the bottom.

Comprehending these ecosystems is incomplete without some appreciation of the powers and need for migration. To me, it is a marvel of nature that this complex process happens so precisely in so many ways. It is beyond the powers of science to create this masterpiece of life. A look at each park individually enhances our appreciation of the wildlife of this unparalleled wilderness.

Glacier Bay

Glacier Bay National Park and Preserve harbors marine and terrestrial fauna at home in both the Pacific Ocean and the temperate rain forest. Glacier Bay also offers one of the world's best opportunities to observe the succession of marine and terrestrial fauna following glacial retreat.

A unique feature is its pristine and biologically rich marine ecosystem. While there are many protected land areas in the world, there are few protected marine areas of significant size. Marine waters make up nearly one-fifth of the park. This includes more than 125 miles (200 km) of isolated outer coast facing the Gulf of Alaska, and Glacier Bay itself, which extends 60 miles (96 km) inland. Mary Beth Moss, resource manager for Glacier Bay National Park and Preserve, says it is "the largest protected marine system in the world."

The richness of the bay's marine fauna begins with its abundance of phytoplankton. Tremendous glacial runoff, an upwelling of nutrient-rich waters caused by tidal turbulence, and long hours of daylight stimulate blooms of phytoplankton during the summer. Krill and other zooplankton feed on the phytoplankton and, in turn, become prey for invertebrates and some vertebrates.

Invertebrates that thrive in marine waters include shellfish: Dungeness, king and Tanner crab, as well as clams, scallops and shrimp. Fiords with retreating glaciers illustrate how barnacles, mussels, sea stars, urchins, sea cucumbers, sea anemones and a variety of crabs, worms, snails and chitons will recolonize newly available habitat.

Park waters host more than 200 species of fish, including five species of Pacific salmon. Fish associated with subtidal **benthic** communities are the Pacific halibut, rockfish, lingcod, Pacific cod, sablefish and pollock. Small schooling fish found throughout the water column include capelin, sandlance, herring, juvenile walleye pollock, juvenile salmonids and lanternfish.

Glacier Bay has recorded about 220 bird species including many seabirds, shorebirds and waterfowl that depend on the marine

A male blue grouse courts a female in the Bartlett Cove rain forest. (Matthew Cahill)

ecosystem. Because of the abundance of aquatic prey, thousands of seabirds nest on nearby islands, cliffs and rocky shores. The Marble Islands and cliffs adjacent to Margerie Glacier have the largest seabird colonies, hosting black-legged kittiwakes, pelagic cormorants, mew and glaucous-winged gulls, and the ever popular tufted and horned puffins. The black oyster-catcher is common on gravel beaches. Glacier Bay may also have the largest concentration of marbled murrelet, a species that is now listed as threatened in the Lower 48, as well as Kittlitz's murrelet. Common, Pacific and red-throated loons and large rafts of surf, white-winged and black scoters, harlequin ducks and common and red-breasted mergansers feed in the upper bay throughout the summer. One of my lasting memories of the upper bay is not only seeing the abundant bird life but frequently hearing the whistle of wings as ducks whiz by. In late summer, large flocks of migrating geese and sea ducks find refuge here. Much to their surprise, park biologists have also found perhaps the largest concentrations of red-necked phalaropes, a shorebird, migrating through at this time.

Marine mammals, including the endangered humpback whale and the threatened Steller sea lion, also count on the bay for food. [**Editor's note:** Biologists separate Alaska's sea lions into eastern and western stocks. Sea lions in the eastern Gulf are listed as threatened, those to the west as endangered.] The sight of a hump-back whale, weighing tens of tons, bursting from the surface of the bay and of grunting sea lions basking at a haulout on Marble Island etch Glacier Bay into the mind of any visitor. What may be the largest population of harbor seals in Alaska breed and nurture their pups on

the floating ice near tidewater glaciers. Minke and killer whales, as well as harbor and Dall's porpoises, feed in near-shore waters. Boaters cruising the lower bay and Cross Sound can spot sea lions dodging hunting killer whales by keeping the boat between themselves and the larger predators. Sea otters are beginning to recolonize Glacier Bay as well as nearby Icy Strait and Cross Sound, much to the delight of visitors who are invariably attracted to this mammal that eats more crab and shrimp in a day than many of us could afford all year.

The park's inventory of terrestrial fauna

The immense size of the world heritage wilderness allows viable ecosystems to operate with little disturbance from people. Here predator/prey relationships follow a more natural cycle. Chief among predators are wolves and bears, populations of which are healthy within the wilderness. (George Wuerthner)

includes a wide range of land birds. Such northern breeders as the arctic tern and parasitic jaeger find barren outwash plains ideal nesting habitat. Common to the mature forest at Bartlett Cove is the blue grouse and numerous songbirds: ruby-crowned kinglet, hermit thrush, Swainson's thrush, varied thrush, robin and Wilson's warbler for example. Songbirds are more numerous and diverse where there is mature forest. Their numbers dwindle in the barren upper reaches of the bay, although I have observed fox sparrow, pine siskin, orange-crowned warbler, gray-cheeked thrush and hermit thrush here.

Of the 28 species of land mammals in the park, perhaps the most unique is the glacier bear, a rare bluish color phase of the black bear. Some of the more mobile species of mammals, such as the mountain goat and brown bear, have moved into recently unglaciated terrain and moose have expanded their range into newly vegetated areas where willows abound. River otter, marten, mink and weasel are widespread, while the scarcer wolverine is present though rarely sighted. Expanding vegetation has attracted a variety of rodents including marmot, porcupine and several species of voles, shrews and mice. The Alsek River delta provides habitat for lynx, snowshoe hare and beaver, species that have reached the coast from the interior using the river corridor.

Tatshenshini-Alsek

Tatshenshini-Alsek Wilderness Provincial Park is noted for its abundance of large predators: wolves, wolverine and particularly brown/grizzly bears. The wide, thinly vegetated, gravel floodplains and numerous glacial outwash plains on the Tatshenshini and Alsek rivers make these wilderness monarchs more visible to rafters. We saw several brown and black bears on our float trip down the "Tat," and looked unsuccessfully for a glacier bear, found nowhere else in Canada.

Although uncommon in British Columbia, about 200 Dall sheep, roughly half the province's total population, inhabit steep terrain here. Not far away in the Atlin area are stone sheep, a brown color phase of Dall sheep.

Because of their tan color, stone sheep more closely resemble the Rocky Mountain sheep found farther south.

Despite its fast, silty waters, the Tatshenshini River seems to have a surprising abundance of beaver and I frequently saw beaver-chiseled stumps along the riverbank. Beaver are associated with a microscopic, aquatic animal that can give humans a bad case of diarrhea, sometimes called "beaver fever," if its cyst is ingested. The cyst of giardia thrives in slow-moving waters, such as beaver ponds. Perhaps because these ponds offer some of the limited sources of silt-free water, a number of rafters who have turned to the ponds for water have suffered from this debilitating parasite.

Tatshenshini-Alsek Wilderness Provincial Park not only has a transitional climate but also a transitional ecosystem. Because the park is close to the northern extension of Rocky Mountain ecosystems, its 44 species of mammals include the woodchuck, seen only rarely in Kluane and not at all in the Alaska parks, and the least chipmunk, a species more common in southerly areas and absent from the other parks.

The diversity of its bird life reinforces the transitional nature of this park. Only here live the four species of grouse native to the region: spruce, blue, ruffed and sharp-tailed. The park supports 218 species of birds. Some species of songbirds have reached the northern and western limits of their range and are not found in the other parks. For example, I frequently observed magnolia warbler in the shrubs along the riverbank. However, this warbler doesn't seem to have penetrated the coastal mountains, a necessary feat for it to populate similar habitat in Glacier Bay National Preserve.

Kluane

Kluane National Park has some of the richest and most diverse wildlife habitat in northern Canada. The combination of coastal, arctic, alpine, northern prairie and Siberian steppe ecosystems enhances its suitability for a variety of species.

If just one species symbolizes the outstanding ecological features of Kluane, it is the Dall sheep. Interest in protecting the Kluane

Omnivorous, black bears occur throughout forested areas, where this one is swatting at alders. (John Hyde/Wild Things)

area began in the early 1900s because of its spectacular mountain scenery and abundance of Dall sheep. About 4,000 roam the park where it is the most numerous large mammal. Sage is important to the Dall sheep's diet, and its profusion in Kluane contributes to high populations of sheep. Other factors include having relatively light snowfall, because it is in the rain shadow of the St. Elias Mountains, and plenty of wind-blown slopes in the winter, which exposes forage.

While much of the park is not easily accessible, one of the largest concentrations of sheep occurs at Sheep Mountain, right beside the Alaska Highway. When I drive west from Haines Junction and reach the crest of the hill just before Kluane Lake, I am always stunned by the split image of the beautiful azure lake and perfectly shaped Sheep Mountain. This postcard setting is home to about 300 sheep and Park Service staff have set up spotting scopes at Sheep Mountain Visitor Centre to watch the animals. During midsummer, however, the sheep climb to greener pastures at higher elevations and may be out of view from the highway.

Another denizen of Kluane is the grizzly bear. Scientists believe that the grizzly population in Kluane is one of the most genetically diverse because of its proximity, in each direction, to other well-established populations. When populations are thriving, individuals leave to establish new territories, contributing to genetic diversity. Although the density of bears here is not as great as in coastal areas, the 18 percent of the park that has suitable habitat is highly productive for an interior environment.

Woodland caribou range through Kluane but are not found in the three other parks. The territory of the Burwash herd includes part of the Kluane Range and a plateau on the north side of the Alaska Highway. Woodland caribou are larger than their barrenground relatives but the distinction between the subspecies is slight.

Kluane has 45 species of mammals of which three are rare; woodchuck, northern flying squirrel and heather vole. Sometimes mule deer and cougar, more typical of ecosystems farther south, are seen. In 1986, wood bison were introduced in the Nisling River watershed north of Kluane and small herds occasionally wander by, but this species is not yet on the park checklist.

Kluane has at least 180 species of birds, 118

of which nest here. These species include most of the songbirds expected of the boreal forest as well as some, the mountain bluebird for example, that have reached the northern and western extent of their range. If climate is warming, as some scientists speculate, the ranges of these birds will probably expand farther north and west. Kluane itself has few lakes or wetlands, so not many waterfowl inhabit the park, but nearby areas, such as the Shakwak Trench, contain abundant nesting habitat for ducks, geese and swans and shorebirds.

Kluane lists only 10 species of fish: arctic grayling, rainbow trout, lake trout, Dolly Varden, northern pike, burbot, pygmy and round whitefish, slimy sculpin and kokanee. The kokanee, the only naturally occurring population of landlocked red salmon in the Yukon, inhabits the Kathleen Lake area that drains into the Alsek River. Scientists think this population of fish was anadromous until Lowell Glacier blocked the Alsek. The fish were not able to migrate out to sea any longer and adapted instead to migrate to nearby Sockeye Lake to spawn. The park no longer has any anadromous fish, but outside the park the Kluane River, which drains Kluane Lake, has a run of chums that attracts grizzly bears in late fall.

Wrangell-St. Elias

Wrangell-St. Elias National Park and Preserve and Kluane National Park amount to one contiguous natural system. Accordingly, both parks share some of the same reasons for being a World Heritage Site, such as abundant populations of Dall sheep. Since it is nearly two and a half times larger than Kluane and has more

area free of glaciers and icefields, Wrangell-St. Elias also has a larger population of sheep, estimated by park biologists to number between 13,000 and 20,000. There may be three to four times as many sheep as moose, although comprehensive surveys of wildlife populations within the park/preserve have yet to be funded. Dall sheep, as well as mountain goats in the coastal mountains, are hunted for meat and trophies in the preserve where hunting is allowed.

The northern portion of Wrangell-St. Elias also has the largest population of caribou, in three herds, in this world heritage wilderness. The smaller Chisana and Mentasta herds, about 500 animals each, spend most of their annual cycle within the park/preserve; the larger Nelchina herd migrates through from summer to winter range.

Plains bison were introduced to some river valleys carpeted with grasslands in 1950. These bison are not as suited for this habitat as the wood bison near Kluane, but more than 100 animals have survived in two small herds in the Chitina drainage.

Thriving populations of hooved mammals are preyed on by large carnivores in places where predators continue to be a functional part of the ecosystem. Both wolves and brown bears appear to have healthy populations, although studies have not been conducted to confirm this observation by park biologists.

Forty species of land mammals roam Wrangell-St. Elias from carnivores, such as coyote, red fox, wolverine and lynx, to smaller mammals like rodents. Nowhere else outside Alaska and the Yukon does the abundance and diversity of native species of mammals flourish so well within viable ecosystems.

The list of 214 species of birds recorded here contains species typical of interior and coastal Alaska. The park/preserve encompasses some of the plateau near Glennallen that has many small lakes, which attract the world's largest concentration of nesting trumpeter swans. As with mammal predators, avian hunters are numerous and diverse. Plenty of cliffs provide good nesting habitat for raptors such as hawks and owls, and an abundance of nesting trees sustains a healthy population of bald eagles.

FACING PAGE:
Although interior waterways are often loaded with glacial silt, coastal waters offer good fishing for species such as halibut and salmon. (Bob Butterfield)

LEFT:
The 20 legs of the Pycnopodia *or sunflower star, make it the fastest sea star on earth. Excursion Inlet, easternmost inlet of Glacier Bay National Park, abounds with these creatures. (Scott Croll)*

Wrangell-St. Elias has 22 species of fish: The five species of Pacific salmon and freshwater fish such as Dolly Varden, lake trout, cutthroat trout, arctic grayling, burbot, round whitefish and humpback whitefish that are especially attractive to anglers.

The World Heritage Site has a collage of habitats typical of a subarctic environment, which contributes to the diversity of wildlife that exists here. Besides being enjoyable to observe, the abundance and diversity of wildlife that populates the four parks provide excellent examples of how animals adapt to challenging environmental conditions. ▲

PHANTOM OF THE FOREST

In the still of the northern summer twilight, deep within the forest of the World Heritage Site, a small, silent, ghostlike creature swoops down from the top of a dead birch. Its grayish-white, rectangular body deftly makes two sharp turns, avoiding a web of limbs that obstructs its glide. As the figure comes closer, a dark tail can be seen, dangling from four outstretched legs; its front legs connected to its back legs by a flap of furry skin. Just before it appears that this creature might crash into the base of a nearby white spruce, it swoops up, extends its legs forward, and lands softly, clinging to the bark of the tree. So enters the northern flying squirrel.

What comes as a surprise to even those familiar with most of Alaska's wildlife is that the northern flying squirrel not only resides in the state's coniferous forests, but that it is fairly common. In fact, it is nearly as common as its diurnal cousin, the red squirrel. Although the northern flying squirrel and red squirrel share the same habitat, sources of food, and sometimes even the same trees, they do not share the night. At dusk, when red

squirrels begin retiring to their dens, flying squirrels quietly emerge from shelters hidden in the canopy. Because of its little known presence and ghostlike suspension in the air when it is seen, the flying squirrel is truly the phantom of the forest.

The flying squirrel scurries to the other side of the thick tree trunk after landing, shielding itself from a possible predator, such as a great horned owl, that might be following close behind. The squirrel clings to the huge spruce for a moment, checking for possible danger. Large eyes that bulge from the sides of its head provide excellent night vision and a wide peripheral view of its surroundings.

Satisfied that no danger lurks, the squirrel twitches nervously and quickly climbs to the first large branch several feet above the ground. It takes a few steps onto the branch and appears to do a couple of push-ups, but is really surveying the next glide path. Then with a strong push from its legs, the squirrel leaps

Using its claws, a juvenile flying squirrel holds its place more than 60 feet (18 m) up on a white spruce trunk. (Jim Grace)

The flying squirrel has a strong ropelike muscle on each side of its body that holds the edge of the patagium taut, allowing it to perform much like a hang glider's wings. A slender rod of cartilage parallel to each forearm and attached to the flying squirrel's wrist extends out, offering more surface area for gliding. The tail provides balance, giving the squirrel more airfoil and longer glides. Most glides cover a distance of 20 to 60 feet (6 m to 18 m), but glides as long as 300 feet (91 m) down steep slopes have been observed.

Descending at a 30-degree angle, the squirrel glides a short distance to another large spruce. It lands, quickly turns around, and then scampers, headfirst, down the trunk. The squirrel runs across the forest floor to a nearby midden of chewed-up spruce cones that red squirrels have accumulated during the years. Buried within this 2-foot (60 cm) pile of debris are some of the cones that the current red squirrel neighbor stashed over the summer. As the growing season comes to an end and other sources of food dwindle, the spruce seeds will be important food for the red squirrel and, to a lesser degree, the flying squirrel.

After taking a few sniffs here and there, the flying squirrel scoots off, knowing there are more attractive sources of food available this time of year, mushrooms and truffles. These fungi are a prime component of the flying squirrel's diet during late summer. Besides being a good source of carbohydrates and minerals, mushrooms and truffles are 70 to 80 percent water. Since this squirrel doesn't have a pond or stream in the immediate vicinity, fungi serve as a thirst-quenching substitute for the lack of a reliable water supply.

The hungry squirrel rustles through dead leaves and needles on the forest floor. Beneath the floor lies a network of filaments (hyphae) that belong to various species

again into the dark, immediately assuming a Superman pose. All of its appendages are extended and its cape, a flap of skin called a patagium, is outstretched.

of fungi. The hyphae weave through the organic layer of soil, allowing the fungi to feed off plant matter as either a saprophyte (feeding on dead plants) or a parasite (feeding from a live host). The sporocarp, or fruiting body, of some saprophytes grows above ground. These sporocarps are more commonly called mushrooms. When late summer rains begin, a profusion of colorful mushrooms bursts through the damp forest floor. There are red-capped amanita, delicious orange and golden pholiota. All of these, even the poisonous amanita, nourish both flying squirrels and red squirrels.

But the delicacy that the flying squirrel favors is truffles, the underground sporocarp from a type of parasitic fungi called mycorrhiza. Mycorrhizal fungi have a symbiotic relationship with plant roots, particularly trees in the pine family. The relationship is so close that the hyphae from the fungi not only intertwine around the roots of the plant, but actually penetrate the cell wall of the root tips. This allows the mycorrhizal fungi to exchange nutrients and water, which it easily absorbs from the soil, for sugars that the host photosynthetically produces. Unlike the host, fungi have

enzymes that dissolve the mineral content of the soil allowing nutrients to be readily absorbed within its cells. Unlike fungi, the needles or leaves of the host have chlorophyll and exposure to sunlight, essential ingredients for photosynthesis. Together, they each get what is needed to survive.

The symbiotic relationship becomes more complex. If mycorrhizal fungi are to successfully propagate, the spores in the underground sporocarps need to be dispersed aboveground. To enlist help, as the sporocarp matures, it gives off a strong odor. The flying squirrel, with its keen sense of smell, is able to locate these nuggets of nutrition buried in the soil. In addition to its nutritional constituents, the sporocarp contains spores, nitrogen-fixing bacteria and yeast, which are not digested by the squirrel. When the squirrel excretes this material, the spores are not only deposited in a new place, but encased in the bacteria and yeast. The fecal pellet ultimately becomes a fertilized bed for the spores.

Witches broom, a type of parasite, offers a suitable nesting site for a northern flying squirrel. (Jim Grace)

The flying squirrel briefly stops its scampering to defecate. As it turns out, the

fecal pellet is deposited right next to a seedling white spruce. Little does this animal realize

A flying squirrel eats a truffle, the underground fruit of a fungi. Flying squirrels and fungi play a crucial role in the health of a forest. (Jim Grace)

the significance of this occurrence for future generations of flying squirrels. Fungi spores from truffles that the squirrel ate the other day are embedded in the fecal pellet. These spores will soon germinate and form a new colony of fungi that become entwined with the roots of the seedling. This will provide the seedling with the nutrients it needs to establish healthy growth. Decades from now, the seedling may become a mature white spruce, providing future generations of flying squirrels with critical habitat.

Although other mammals eat truffles, none have as close an interdependence as the truffle-tree-flying squirrel triad. Considering the important role it plays in forest regeneration, Rocky the Flying Squirrel is probably a more appropriate symbol of forest health than Smokey the Bear.

The odor of truffles comes seeping through the forest floor. The squirrel sniffs here and there and then furiously starts digging with its front paws. Just beneath the surface is a walnut-sized truffle. The squirrel, squatting on its hind legs, holds the truffle with its front paw and quickly devours the delicacy. It then scurries off looking for additional breakfast items.

Besides fungi, the summer diet for flying squirrels includes berries and the new growth of needles at the tips of conifer branches. But the flying squirrel is not strictly a vegetarian. Being an opportunistic omnivore, it will eat insect grubs and larvae, bird eggs, even nestling birds. In the winter, lichens, which are a combination of fungus and algae, comprise most of its diet. Other items include fungi cached by red squirrels, seeds, and nuts from hardwood trees, where available.

After finishing its breakfast, the squirrel takes a couple of short hops to the base of a small spruce, climbs several feet up the trunk to an extended branch, struts out to the end of the bobbing branch, leaps onto the nearby branch of a larger spruce, stops to grab some arboreal lichens hanging from the needles, and then heads up the tree with the lichens in its mouth. About two-thirds the way to the top of the spire is a tangle of twigs.

This is one of several trees on this hillside that has been inflicted with rust, another kind of parasitic fungus. The rust creates a bundle of deformed branches called witches broom. This ball of twigs provides the flying squirrel with the makings for a cozy winter residence. The squirrel burrows into the middle of the witches broom, where it has previously cleared out a small chamber. The lichen is stuffed to the side of the chamber, which will help insulate the squirrel from the below-zero cold that can be expected in just a couple of months. Other insulating materials include mosses, leaves and shredded bark.

In the bitter cold of midwinter, other flying squirrels will visit this witches broom nest. Since fat squirrels don't fly well, flying squirrels don't develop a warm layer of fat for the winter like ground squirrels and other rodents. To compensate, several friendly flying squirrels will cuddle together during the coldest months, sharing not only the insulated den but their body heat. During this time, they will be in a torpid, or lethargic state, but they will not be hibernating.

This is just one of several nests that the squirrel has in its several-acre domain. Nests located in witches broom are used mostly in winter. During summer, the squirrel will nest in the cavities of trees as well as on leafy platforms, called drays. Often, the cavity in snag trees (dead standing trees) was made by another animal, frequently woodpeckers. The drays are usually a bundle of moss, lichens and grass, perched on a limb near the trunk of a spruce. Some drays are built on top of bird nests; others are platforms previously built by red squirrels.

Nest use is changed frequently and having several nests is essential for the squirrel's survival. Sometimes a nest is invaded by a tree-climbing predator such as the pine marten or weasel. When this happens, the squirrel may abandon the nest for a while. Also, flying squirrels get infested with fleas. The nest not only provides a home for the squirrel, but for the fleas as well. Once the nest gets too infested, the squirrel moves to another, leaving most of the fleas behind to perish. Some fleas go with the squirrel, continuing the cycle.

Our foraging squirrel will circle its territory a couple of times during the next few hours. Before the brief night is over, it will have traveled more than a mile, going up and down and back and forth across a several-acre plot that serves as its territory. During the summer, squirrels are more prone to having individual territories. The outer boundary, however, will be shared with other flying squirrels.

This has been a good night for the squirrel. It found an abundant supply of truffles and encountered no predators.

Although they are not uncommon, northern flying squirrels are generally nocturnal and are seen much less often than their relative, the red squirrel. (Jim Grace)

But the squirrel's long-term safety is not so secure. The mature stand of white spruce that dominates the hillside has been targeted for logging. If the white spruce are clearcut, the flying squirrel will not only lose its home but its advantage for self-protection. Its ability to climb and glide helps it escape carnivores. Also, its ability to safely glide through a dense cover of tree branches protects it from other flying creatures, such as hawks and owls.

A young female clings to a biologist's finger. The northern flying squirrel is slightly smaller than the more familiar red squirrel. An adult weighs, on average, 4.9 ounces (140 grams) and is about 12 inches long (30 cm). The underside of the flying squirrel is grayish-white and its upper coat is cinnamon-colored. The coat is shed once a year, beginning in early summer. Breeding in Alaska begins from March to late June, depending on the length and severity of the winter. Gestation requires 37 days. Although flying squirrels in more moderate climates may breed twice a year, in Alaska breeding usually occurs once a year, with two young per litter. Young are fully grown after eight months. The mortality rate during the first year is about 50 percent; few survive more than four or five years. (Jim Grace)

Without the cover of mature trees, it will be more vulnerable to predators.

Lack of forest cover will also change the food supply: The ground will be drier from more exposure to sun and wind, and fungi will dwindle without dampness. While more berries may be available, this sweet food source doesn't offer as much nutrition as fungi.

If logging occurs, the squirrel can relocate to a nearby forested area that may not be logged. But this stand of mature spruce is already occupied by other flying squirrels. Given the complexities of nature, the hillside already has a maximum abundance of flying squirrels. In Interior Alaska, biologists have estimated this as approximately one flying squirrel per seven acres for a closed-canopy forest where mature white spruce predominate. Any reduction in the carrying capacity of the habitat equates to a reduction in the abundance of a species.

But there are alternatives. Clearcutting is not the only option for logging. Other methods retain some of the forest cover and large trees that flying squirrels need for nesting and gliding. Robert Mowery and John Zasada, formerly with the U.S. Forest Service, Institute of Northern Forestry in Fairbanks, said in a 1982 report on the northern flying squirrel in Interior Alaska, "Particular attention should be given to keeping cutting units small and maintaining relatively undisturbed corridors of trees for travel between denning sites and foraging areas. The group-selection silvicultural system [which results in a forest having uneven-age stands] appears to best meet requirements of both squirrel species and needs for regeneration and growth of the trees."

Scientists have only recently understood the importance of the flying squirrel to regeneration of the forest and options that protect the squirrel's

habitat and population would not have been a serious consideration before many foresters began to accept the concept of ecosystem management. This approach to forest management more clearly recognizes the need to main-tain the complex processes of forest ecosystems.

So, because of new information about the forest and its critters, the future of the northern flying squirrel may actually be improving. If so, its preferred haunts, stands of mature and old-growth conifers, will continue to be part of the forest, providing the flying squirrel with the food and shelter it needs to survive. And then, the phantom of the forest will live on. •

The flying squirrel relies on a cape, a flap of skin called a patagium, to allow it to glide from tree to tree. A strong muscle holds the patagium taut, enabling the cape to act much like the wings of a hang glider. (Jim Grace)

The First People

FACING PAGE:

Indigenous people have relied on the rivers for travel and sustenance for centuries. Fish provide Athabaskans with fresh food in summer; smoked or dried fish supplement their winter diet. Here Silas Alexander and stepson Dan Bifelt position a fish wheel, made from spruce saplings, on a river. Baskets on each side, turned by the current, scoop fish into a holding bin. (Colleen Herning-Wickens)

Although one of the hallmarks of this world heritage wilderness is its relative freedom from deep disturbance by man, small groups of people have wandered its more hospitable avenues for thousands of years. The first people of the region were nomadic hunters from Asia who migrated to the New World more than 15,000 years ago, probably by the Bering Land Bridge. Trodding across the wind-blown steppe, the first people followed herds of now mostly extinct large mammals, such as the mammoth, which thrived in this semiarid, grassy habitat. At this time there was no boreal forest and the area that is now coastal rain forest was buried under ice.

Based on linguistic, dental, genetic and archaeological data, scientists currently think that the first people arrived in three independent waves, each from distinct founding populations in Siberia and northeast Asia. The second wave, the NaDene people, relate most directly to this World Heritage Site because they settled several thousand years ago in what is now central Alaska and the Yukon.

As the climate warmed and conditions began to change, a rising sea flooded the land bridge, cutting off further overland migration. The steppe gave way to a boreal forest with animals, such as moose, well-adapted to this type of environment. Glaciers retreated from the coast and up some of the U-shaped valleys, exposing coastal waters and lands to an invasion of pioneering flora and fauna that, through succession, would eventually become a coastal rain forest. Retreat of the glaciers was erratic. Sometimes, instead of warming, the climate cooled for a spell and the glaciers pushed ahead again, burying the advances made by the flora and fauna.

With this climate change, the plants and animals diversified, and so did the NaDene. In time, different tribes evolved, each with different means of subsistence, culture and language. The people who stayed in the boreal forest became Athabaskan (called Dene in Canada); those who followed the melting glaciers and settled in the coastal rain forest became Tlingit; the Eyak, a small tribe, settled in the Copper River delta region.

Once the continental ice sheet melted away, the northern Athabaskan homeland stretched from central Alaska through northern Canada as far east as Hudson's Bay. These people evolved into about 30 groups, each having a different language. Three of the groups, the Ahtna, Upper Tanana and Southern Tutchone, occupied the northern part of the Wrangell-St. Elias region. The Lower Ahtna controlled the upper Copper River basin; the Upper Tanana inhabited the Nabesna and Chisana river valleys; the Southern Tutchone lived in what

Bark huts line the shore of Disenchantment Bay, where Tlingit once gathered to hunt seals. Seal skins are stretched to dry and seal skin containers hold the blubber, which was the fuel for stone lamps. A wick was fashioned of beach grass or a twisted rag. (Photo from the Harriman Alaska Expedition, courtesy of the Heritage Library)

A woman flenses seal skin at Yakutat in 1899. Harbor seals and other marine mammals contributed to a well-developed culture, where abundant food and shelter allowed the people to spend more time in artistic and spiritual endeavors. Natives wove untanned seal and sea lion skin into rope; with beach cobbles they crushed shells and mixed them with seal brains or salmon eggs to make a paste for waterproofing seams of wooden boxes. (Photo from the Harriman Alaska Expedition, courtesy of the Heritage Library)

is now the southwestern corner of the Yukon.

Sitka spruce and western hemlock established roots in the newly exposed coastal areas, and so did the Tlingit. There were 16 or 17 groups in Southeast Alaska, each with cultural differences, speaking three or four languages. Eventually they became more united through trade, war, potlatches and intermarriage. The Tlingit groups in the St. Elias Mountains include the Yakutat, the northernmost group, who lived in the Yakutat Bay area; the Dry Bay people, whose villages, now abandoned, lay at the mouth of the Alsek River; the Hoonah in the Glacier Bay area and the

Chilkat-Chilkoot in the Lynn Canal area.

The Eyak probably descended from Athabaskans about 3,500 years ago, migrating down the Copper River to the delta. Here they developed a more coastal lifestyle and a distinctly different language. They were not a blend of Eskimo and Tlingit, as anthropologists had earlier thought. But competition from the Chugach Eskimo in Prince William Sound to the west and the Yakutat Tlingit to the east, prevented them from spreading much beyond a couple of villages on the delta.

Subsisting

Despite their differences, all tribes remained hunters, fishermen and gatherers; there was no agriculture or domesticated crops. Those who reached the coast, where resources were more abundant, required different tools and skills than those who stayed in the less bountiful Interior. Each band became expert in knowing the resources and the natural cycles of its place. Based on this knowledge, they developed simple but elegant skills, tools and means of transportation to pursue food, shelter and clothing.

The Athabaskans became the people of the boreal forest and of the rivers, using the network of waterways that flow through the northern forest as travel routes. Reliance on the forest continues. In *The Athabaskans: People of the Boreal Forest*, (1983) Richard Nelson says, "The Athabaskan people's daily existence is closely bound to natural events: the changing seasons, the temperamental weather, the transforming landscape, and the ever-important behavior of game.... The use of animals illustrates how tightly Athabaskan technology is integrated with the natural world.... The most

vital and ingenious elements of Athabaskan technology are those used for subsistence: hunting game, trapping animals, and catching fish."

The various Athabaskan groups lived in a similar environment and followed a similar, seminomadic lifestyle. Small bands, consisting of a couple of families at most, would move from one resource to another depending on the season it was available. Those that had an abundant supply of salmon to harvest, such as the Ahtna, could afford to be less nomadic and have larger settlements. Hunting strategies depended on the band's access to moose, sheep or caribou. In winter, bands would split into smaller units and move into half-buried log

Wearing white and hiding their gear under white canvas helped Hoonah sealers camouflage their approach when hunting seals in Glacier Bay. (Photo from the Harriman Alaska Expedition, courtesy of the Heritage Library)

dwellings or skin lodges. Furs were used for clothing and trapping was done mostly in the winter when pelts were prime.

The Tlingit became the sea canoe people. They fashioned from tree trunks a variety of sea-going canoes, which were used extensively for hunting, fishing and trade missions. Besides harvesting marine mammals and halibut from the ocean and salmon from the rivers, the Tlingit picked seaweed, clams and mussels from the beach during low tide. Use of the intertidal area was extensive enough so that it is still said "when the tide is out, the table is set." In addition to the sea, the land provided deer, mountain goat and berries.

The bounty of the sea gave the Tlingit significantly more subsistence options than the Athabaskan, particularly in winter. This allowed the Tlingit to put less time into hunting, fishing and gathering, to form larger bands, and to develop complex social arrangements. The result was the forming of the Raven and Eagle moieties, parts of a tribe having unilateral descent, that dictated social order. Within each moiety were many clans. Each clan built large winter houses that accommodated several families. Houses were made with planks split from large trees that provided not only shelter but a place to display art and family crests. Totem poles adorned the entrance to the house, telling a story about its occupants.

To the Natives, the importance of the natural world transcends just being a vital source of commodities. Their understanding of the natural world and their beliefs about the spiritual world were combined; all things from rocks to plants to animals were alive with spirits. For instance, the raven was both a real thing and a powerful spirit.

Nelson says, "Traditional Athabaskan religion centers around the spirituality and awareness of nature. The animals, plants, earth, and sky are invested with special powers, and humans are duty bound to show their respect. Behavior toward the environment is governed by a code of morality that recognizes nature as the source of all life on which people depend. By following this code (its gestures of respect, conservation of resources, and avoidance of waste), Athabaskans maintain both a spiritual and physical balance with the world around them. Perhaps this is the key to their success in adapting to Alaska's boreal forest and thriving over a history that spans several millennia."

Anthropologist Frederica de Laguna says of the Tlingit, in *Under Mount St. Elias: The History and Culture of the Yakutat Tlingit* (1972), "The ways in which the people make a living, securing their food and clothing, their medicines and luxuries, bring us back again to a further understanding of their environment. These are not simply technological activities, but have moral aspects, men are not something apart from nature, but share with 'animate' and seemingly 'inanimate' things the same being, while 'natural laws' have social, moral and 'supernatural' aspects."

For thousands of years life went on as people followed the retreat of the glaciers and the seasonal cycles of nature. There were occasional wars, and trading took place between bands who exchanged resources they had, for example copper, for resources they lacked, such as furs. Much of the trade was between coastal and inland bands using the Copper and Alsek rivers as trade routes. The Tutchone were often the middleman between the Tlingit and other Athabaskan.

Contact with Westerners

Native contact with western society came slowly at first. Trading introduced Russian goods, such as steel knives and iron cooking pots, to the region well before the actual presence of white men. The goods and stories passed from band to band alerted the indigenous people that other cultures and people existed.

The return of the Vitus Bering expedition to Kamchatka in 1741-1742 brought news to the Europeans of an abundance of sea otters and other furbearers. Russian fur traders started venturing by ship to the Aleutians and the Gulf of Alaska to exploit the sea otter. Because the Russians had more powerful weapons, such as

FACING PAGE:
Charlie Jimmie Sr., a Chilkat dancer, wears a Chilkat blanket during performances representing his people, the Chilkat Tlingit of the Lynn Canal area. (John Hyde/Wild Things)

ABOVE:
Mrs. Marks of Klukwan rolls mountain goat fur into yarn to weave a Chilkat blanket. Highly prized among the Tlingits, Chilkat blankets brought honor to the wearer and to the maker. Traditionally the blankets were not signed and it was not always known who made them. (Staff)

Tlingit carver Rick Beasley carves an octopus at Bartlett Cove. Natives used octopus for bait in halibut fishing. They wrapped a tiny piece of octopus around a hook and tied it with spruce root. (Matthew Cahill)

guns and cannons, they were able to dominate the Aleuts, conscripting many to hunt sea otters. The traders, searching for new sources of fur, moved farther east, reaching the Wrangell-St. Elias region in the 1780s and establishing a post at Yakutat in 1796. The Russian American Co., formed in 1799, soon became the pivotal Russian presence in Alaska.

The arrival of the Russians introduced several deadly diseases for which Native populations had no resistance. Entire villages were nearly wiped out by a smallpox epidemic that began in the 1830s. Disease so decimated the Natives that population estimates by early white explorers were not representative of conditions before contact. Brutal treatment inflicted by some Russians contributed to the reduced population.

Athabaskan and Tlingit villages that were near trading posts resisted the Russians. In 1805, the Yakutat Tlingit destroyed the Russian post established in their area; the Ahtna wiped the Russians out of the Copper River basin in the 1840s. These problems, and the decline in sea otter populations, influenced the Czar's decision to sell Alaska.

The United States bought Alaska from Russia in 1867, assuming full rights of ownership. For decades all this meant was an occasional military or scientific expedition to the territory, trading by the Alaska Commercial Co. that had bought Russian American Co. interests, and a trickle of prospectors searching for gold. The subsistence lifestyle of the Natives was made easier by some of the western products now available to them, but remained essentially unchanged.

However, as the century came to a close large fish canneries were constructed in coastal areas and a gold rush was about to begin in the Yukon's Klondike. A cash economy was establishing roots, and while Natives had long been accustomed to bartering goods, the cash economy provided them with wages for cannery work and for guiding prospectors over the coastal mountains. The cash economy, and the adaptation to it, was probably the most profound change that had confronted them for thousands of years. With currency, wealth was measured by a standard that was tangible, not biodegradable, and easily accumulated; a perspective alien to the traditional subsistence economy. Currency also encouraged saving rather than sharing, also a departure from tradition.

United States interest in the Territory of Alaska increased around the turn of the 20th century. This led to a number of problems with Natives, due primarily to their unresolved status as citizens. There were questions regarding voting rights, land ownership and rights to use natural resources. The battles fought over these issues were not in the forest, as they had been with the Russians, but in the courts and the halls of Alaska's Legislature and the U.S. Congress, an indication of the ability of Natives to adapt to a changing world. Natives lost some battles but essentially won the war and their indigenous rights. Two milestone pieces of federal legislation important to the World Heritage Site are the Alaska Native Claims Settlement Act (ANCSA), passed in 1971, and the Alaska National Interest Lands Conservation Act (ANILCA), passed in 1980.

The purpose of ANCSA was far-ranging but aimed primarily to assimilate Alaska Natives into the economic mainstream of the United States. To avoid a reservation system, the act took a business approach to settlement and established 13 regional profit corporations with non-profit counterparts for managing social programs. Each Alaska Native born before the act took effect was a shareholder in one of the regional profit corporations. ANCSA also established 203 village corporations in eligible Native villages. The highlight of ANCSA was a settlement of 44 million acres of federal land and $962.5 million in cash to be conveyed to the corporations.

Two Native regional corporations manage lands in the Copper River-Wrangells area: Ahtna Corp. in the Copper River basin and Chugach Alaska Corp. for the Prince William Sound area including the Copper River delta. Although Chugach Alaska Corp. is primarily Eskimo, it incorporates the Eyak. Several smaller village corporations operate in the Copper River basin, including Chistochina, Chitina, Copper Center, Gakona and Gulkana. Eyak is the only village corporation on the Copper River delta. The Native corporations

The late Harry Marvin of Hoonah wears heirlooms of his Tlingit family. Hoonah Tlingits hunted, fished and gathered plant materials from the Glacier Bay area. Their home village lies across Icy Strait from the southern end of the world heritage wilderness. (Staff)

Salmon hang to dry in Klukshu, a Canadian First Nations village whose people used the Kluane and Tatshenshini-Alsek area. These inland people developed a lifestyle substantially different from those living along the coast, where resources were more plentiful. (George Matz)

combined own more than 700,000 acres within the boundaries of Wrangell-St. Elias National Park and Preserve. The Sealaska Corp. is the regional Native corporation for the Glacier Bay area. The two village corporations in this vicinity are Yakutat and Hoonah, neither of which have land claims within Glacier Bay National Park and Preserve.

The origin of ANILCA begins with a section of ANCSA that said 80 million acres of federal land in Alaska should be designated as parks or wildlife refuges. When this section was finally addressed in the late 1970s, an issue of Native subsistence rights arose, something not adequately covered by ANCSA. ANILCA provides subsistence rights, although the actual implementation remains unresolved. Nevertheless, ANILCA is a significant factor in the management of both Wrangell-St. Elias and Glacier Bay national parks and preserves.

First Nations' (the Canadian equivalent of Alaska Natives) rights are protected by the Canadian Constitution, which is now being applied to the management of Kluane National Park and Tatshenshini-Alsek Wilderness Provincial Park. In 1993, the Champagne and Aishihik First Nations signed an agreement with Kluane National Park assuring their right to a subsistence harvest as well as comanagement of the park. Comanagement gives the First Nation people a percentage of the guiding trips on the Alsek River, which begins in Kluane. A similar claim is being worked out with the Kluane First Nation in the western part of the park. The Champagne and Aishihik First Nations also have a comanagement agreement with Tatshenshini-Alsek Wilderness Provincial Park.

Today the Athabaskan and Tlingit are the principal residents of villages in their respective areas. The Eyak still exist, but barely. While goods and services available from an industrial economy have lessened the fickleness of nature's cycles and reduced the rigors of a subsistence lifestyle, many Natives retain a strong attachment to the land and water. In essence, the descendants of the first people have continued to adapt, learning how to survive in a cash economy but retaining a link to subsistence traditions of the past.

Although the World Heritage Site primarily recognizes the dynamic geological and ecological features within each of the parks, the adaptations by its indigenous people are an important cultural corollary worthy of international recognition. While there are no great monuments or structures to recognize these adaptations, the lack of such extravagance is how these cultures survived; they lived by

Tlingits carved this trail marker on a conifer in Glacier Bay, following a practice long established among their people. (George Matz)

simplicity, spirituality and stewardship. Some Native corporation resource development practices may appear to contradict these principles. For instance, the amount of timber harvested has, in some instances, exceeded sustained-yield levels to liquidate natural resources and quickly generate cash. But it has yet to be demonstrated that these new practices will endure. Meanwhile, the World Heritage Site represents not only an intriguing example of geological and biological processes, but of cultural adaptation as well. ▲

Western Explorers Arrive

During the 1700s, European explorers sought to discover parts of the New World unknown to them and, in many instances, lay claim to vast expanses of land based not on familiarity, but just knowing it was there. Although they certainly expected to encounter indigenous people, some Europeans tended to consider indigenous rights subordinate to their own claims. But not all were like this. Some explorers were naturalists, more interested in scientific discoveries than in gaining wealth. Instead of gold or furs, they sought new landscapes, new species of plants and animals, and even new cultures.

The first Europeans to venture to the North Pacific were members of the Bering expedition of 1741-1742. Leaving Petropavlovsk on Siberia's Kamchatka Peninsula on June 4, 1741, Capt.-Cmdr. Vitus Bering set sail for the North Pacific with two ships, the St. Peter and the St. Paul. Sponsored by the Czar of Russia, the expedition sought to determine if a land bridge existed between North America and Siberia and to look into possible mineral wealth. For the latter objective, Bering enlisted German naturalist George Wilhelm Steller, who knew minerals as well as botany, zoology, medicine and ethnography. The two did not share the same goals, a difference that led to tensions on the voyage.

The expedition had endured hardships, including the death of Bering while his crew spent a miserable winter on an isolated island, now Bering Island, in the Commander group west of the Aleutians. But there were accomplishments. On July 15, 1741, the St. Paul sighted land near Dixon Entrance. The same day, Steller, on the St. Peter, sighted the peak that is now Mount St. Elias. However, the crew did not trust Steller's observation since he was not a seaman, and did not record the sighting until the next day when it was clearly visible.

Because of the winds, Bering was not able to head directly for land but drifted north, reaching Kayak Island, east of the Copper River delta, on July 20. Anxious to begin the return trip, Bering allowed only Steller and a few of the crew enough time on Kayak Island to replenish the ship's water supply. In the hours he had, Steller was able to collect a few plants and birds, including a species new to science, the Steller's jay, and to come across a Native camp apparently deserted when the ship approached. He noted that the camp resembled those of Kamchatka Natives, speculating that they might be descendants. Despite his new scientific findings, Steller was forever disappointed at not being allowed more than a few hours to explore.

Reports carried back to Siberia of the abundance of sea otters and fur seals attracted

This forest of what John Muir called "fossilized wood" greeted members of the Harriman Alaska Expedition in 1899 at Glacier Bay. The forest was covered by ice during a glacial advance. Trunks were encased in ice, and many remained standing when glaciers began to retreat from the area about 200 years ago. (Photo from the Harriman Alaska Expedition, courtesy of the Heritage Library)

Russian fur traders, who sought to exploit this wealth. This led to Russian domination in Alaska for more than a century, a presence that severely impacted Native populations as well as some marine mammal and bird populations. Entire villages died out. The large Steller's sea cow, related to manatees and dugongs, and the nearly flightless spectacled cormorant, both easy sources of food for ship's crews, became extinct during this period. The sea otter almost followed. Russian interests in fur spread through Cook Inlet, the Gulf of Alaska, and eventually into the Interior.

Other Western explorers of the Gulf of Alaska were looking for the elusive Northwest Passage to the Atlantic Ocean. One of the most famous voyages was led by Capt. James Cook, the English explorer on his third and last cruise. In 1778, Cook sailed across the Gulf of Alaska but landed only at Kayak Island. In July 1786, Cmdr. Jean Francois de Galaup de La Perouse, on a French-sponsored scientific voyage of the world, anchored in Lituya Bay to investigate the natural history and ethnology of the area. His contacts with Natives were friendly and La Perouse was able to provide some of most complete early scientific observations of Tlingit culture. Ships from later voyages came and went with not much impact on the land other than mapping and naming prominent landscape features.

Inland, Alexander Mackenzie was the first

explorer to cross the continent. In 1789, with a small party of Indians and voyageurs, he left Canada's Lesser Slave Lake by canoe to explore a river that would later be named for him. He hoped to find a route to the Pacific but reached the Beaufort Sea instead. On an expedition starting in 1792, he followed the Fraser River in British Columbia to the Pacific. He did not reach the Wrangell-St. Elias area but did blaze an inland approach to this country.

In 1840, Robert Campbell, a fur trader for the Hudson's Bay Co., became the first European to explore what is now the Yukon. The Hudson's Bay Co. built Fort Selkirk at the confluence of the Pelly and Yukon rivers in 1848 and began competing with the Russians for furs. Campbell discovered gold in 1850 at Fort Selkirk. While this did not spawn a rush, it did attract a trickle of prospectors. The fort was destroyed by the Chilkat Indians in 1852.

The United States purchased Alaska from Russia in 1867. Although some considered the purchase a waste, calling it "Seward's Folly," there was interest in knowing what was up there. In 1870, William Dall, a respected scientist, began surveying the Wrangell-St. Elias region and collecting specimens of minerals, plants, animals and Native culture. Famed naturalist John Muir explored Glacier Bay in 1879 for the first time. A new type of explorer appeared in 1884 when the Pacific Coast Steamship Co., which had been delivering mail to Southeast Alaska ports for several years, began catering to tourists. There were 1,650 tourists the first summer and more each year. The tourists had a craving for Native arts and crafts, which the Tlingit were quick to recognize.

In 1885, Lt. Henry Allen led a three-man

Geologist Israel Cook Russell was the first U.S. Geological Survey scientist sent to Alaska. In 1890 and 1891 he explored and mapped Malaspina Glacier, Yakutat Bay and the Mount St. Elias region, making attempts both years to climb the mountain. Russell fiord and glacier, and Russell Island in Glacier Bay are named for him. (U.S. Geological Survey)

party on an exploration that ranks with the Lewis and Clark expedition. Starting in March, when the river was still locked in ice, Allen's party made it up the Copper River with considerable help from the Ahtna. The party mapped the country, noted its natural history and Native culture, and looked unsuccessfully for copper, discerning from Native tools that there were deposits in the area. Allen also estimated the heights and named many of the highest peaks in the Wrangell Mountains. His party reached the upper Copper River basin and in early June crossed over the Alaska Range

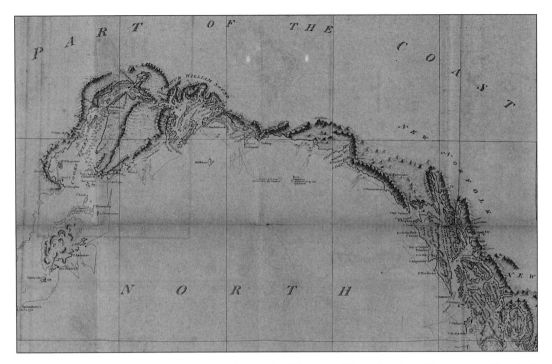

From April to August 1794, Capt. George Vancouver with the ships Discovery and Chatham surveyed the world heritage wilderness coast. This map, prepared following that expedition, shows his route. Vancouver designated the great bay east of Malaspina Glacier Bering Bay, in honor of Vitus Bering. Today the bay is known by its Indian name, Yakutat, but many of the names assigned by Vancouver are still used. (From George Vancouver's A Voyage of Discovery to the North Pacific Ocean and round the World, A New Edition, *(1801); courtesy of The Alaska Collection, Anchorage Municipal Libraries)*

into the Tanana River basin. They then floated down the Tanana and Yukon rivers, making further observations, until they reached St. Michael on the Bering Sea in September, from where they returned home by ship.

In the Yukon, the white population, mostly prospectors and outfitters, had become significant enough for the Canadian government to declare the area a provisional district of the Northwest Territories in 1895. This led to establishment of a government and law enforcement in the Yukon just before the gold rush started. The next year, George Carmack and two companions, Skookum Jim and Tagish (Dawson) Charlie, struck gold near the mouth of the Klondike River. The rest is often told history.

The Dalton Trail, one of the routes to the Klondike Gold Rush, passed through the head-waters of the Tatshenshini River, but neither this trail nor any of the others had much of a lasting influence on any of the four parks. Perhaps the most lasting impact occurred after the Klondike Gold Rush played out when some dedicated prospectors, still looking for their bonanza, drifted into the Wrangell and St. Elias mountains. Some gold was found, and tent cities briefly sprung up, but nothing to match Dawson City. A few old cabins in places like Chisana, site of Alaska's last major gold rush in 1913, record this history.

The U.S. Geological Survey and U.S. Army sponsored a number of expeditions to the Wrangell Mountains to search for minerals and to map the area. Their accomplishments provided prospectors with the information needed to spur mineral development. In 1899, gold was discovered on Jacksina Creek and rich pieces of copper ore were found in the glacial moraine of Kennecott Glacier. A year later, prospectors traced these pieces to Bonanza Ridge, on which was located one of five mines that supplied copper and silver ore to the Kennecott mill.

The Kennecott mines went into full production in 1911 when the 196-mile-long (313.6 km) railroad from Cordova was completed. In 27 years of operation, more than a billion pounds of ore valued at $100 million to $300 million were hauled out by the railroad. By 1931, the rich copper ores were exhausted and the Great Depression sweeping the country was taking its toll. The mine and the railroad were completely abandoned in 1938. The Kennecott mill and the mines on the ridges that supported the mill are now under the jurisdiction of the National Park Service; however, many private inholdings remain within the park's boundaries. The railroad bed is now the McCarthy Road, which traverses the central part of Wrangell-St. Elias National Park and Preserve. Gold discoveries in the Nabesna area led to construction of the Nabesna Road in the early 1930s. This road now provides access to the northern part of the park.

These highlights illustrate an important difference between development of the Wrangell and St. Elias mountains and other frontiers settled by white cultures. The early emphasis here was on the exploitation of furs and minerals, neither activities having the kind of long-term ties to the land that ranching and farming have had in the West. The few white settlements that did develop, such as McCarthy, went boom then bust, leaving only a handful of stragglers behind. As a result, the area has never been very populated, not even when compared to other mountainous areas that are not conducive to dense human settlement. For instance Nepal, which is considered sparsely populated and is not much bigger than the World Heritage Site and adjoining protected land, has a population of more than 20 million people.

Because of its lack of human population, the region remains mostly in a natural state. Today, this allows adventuresome people to discover what is special about a vast expanse of wilderness that has spectacular scenery and an abundance of fish and wildlife. Perhaps this is the long-term destiny of the World Heritage Site. ▲

The Copper River, here lined with fish wheels scooping red salmon, bounds the world heritage wilderness on the west. Lt. Henry Allen and his party traveled this corridor on their epic journey from Prince William Sound across the mountains to the Tanana drainage, downriver to the Yukon then down the Yukon to the Bering Sea. (Jon R. Nickles)

The Adventurers

Because of its contrasts in landscape, climate, scenery and wildlife, the Wrangell-St. Elias region offers a challenging variety of wilderness recreation, each having an element that developed tourist facilities typically don't have — adventure. The thrill of ascending high mountain peaks, skiing or hiking across isolated valleys, kayaking a remote fiord, or rafting down turbulent rivers cannot be experienced at any risk-free theme park or captured by any virtual reality portrayal. "Being there" is as much a lure as "because it's there." For those seeking outdoor challenges, or even the vicarious stimulus of mixing with those who do, the Wrangell-St. Elias-Glacier Bay country is as good as it gets.

The attraction of the region goes a long way back. Early European explorers must have been seeking adventure as well as riches. It would have been easier and less dangerous to acquire wealth closer to home. Early scientists who sought to discover new knowledge about geology, biology and ethnology seemed to have been attracted to risks as well. John Muir, one of the icons of this era, was certainly adventurous.

In the 1880s, something new, tourists, began trickling into the region. Wealthy tourists on Pacific Coast Steamship cruises were interested in novelty and in visiting exotic places, such as Glacier Bay and Yakutat. The ultimate natural history trip, even by today's standards, was the Harriman Alaska Expedition. In the summer of 1899, railroad magnate Edward H. Harriman funded a summer cruise for family and friends that went from Seattle, up the Inside Passage to Glacier Bay, Yakutat, Prince William Sound and on to Siberia. Invited on the expedition were distinguished scientists, writers and artists who documented the trip and presented lectures to the passengers on natural history. Even if these cruises were more luxurious than rigorous, considering the risk of plying these mostly uncharted waters, they were adventurous for their era.

Mountain climbers began appearing here near the turn of the 20th century, attempting to be the first to ascend some of the great peaks. After a couple of unsuccessful attempts by others to climb 18,008-foot (5,462 m) Mount St. Elias, Italian Prince Luigi Amedeo Di Savoia led an elaborately outfitted expedition on a 56-day trek that reached the summit on July 13, 1897. A successful climbing party led by Robert Dunn reached the summit of 14,163-foot (4,296 m) Mount Wrangell in 1909. Thus began a slow but steady progression of expeditions to climb the highest peaks in the Wrangell and St. Elias mountains, including Mount Logan, first scaled in 1925.

Big game hunters also started arriving in the

A bridge over the Kennicott River has made getting to McCarthy, to the Kennicott mill site up the road from McCarthy and into the backcountry much easier. Formerly, residents and visitors had to pull themselves across the river on a hand tram. (Curvin Metzler)

region in search of trophy sheep, caribou, mountain goat, moose and bear. In 1919, a hunting party that included George O. Young, who would later become a West Virginia state senator, began an extraordinary journey that left McCarthy on horseback in early August and arrived in Whitehorse two months later. Eventually, Young wrote a book, *Alaskan-Yukon*

Trophies Won and Lost, about this perilous adventure. When the book was published in 1947, it became a classic among hunters and helped bolster Alaska's image as a hunting paradise. By then, Young had become an avid wildlife photographer and a leading conservationist in his home state.

These early adventurers were the start of

what now supports a small but growing adventure-based industry. Today, visitors from faraway places as well as from Alaska and the Yukon come to the world heritage parks for a healthy dose of adventure. They come to experience the wild of the wilderness, an opportunity that is becoming increasingly endangered. As a German woman I met on a trail in Kluane said, while gazing at the mountain wilderness that surrounded her, "This is a different world here."

Compared to a century ago, today's visitor to this corner of Alaska and Canada has many more travel options from which to choose. Opportunities for wildlife viewing, mountain climbing, skiing, hiking, whitewater rafting and kayaking exist here.

Many climbing expeditions head for Kluane and Wrangell-St. Elias parks. But the high elevations, extensive glaciers and severe weather require good mountaineering skills. About 150 people a year attempt to climb peaks in the Icefield Range in Kluane, with each trip averaging 20 days. Mount Logan, the highest peak in Canada, is the most popular climb. Top attractions in Wrangell-St. Elias park are Sanford, Blackburn, Bona and St. Elias, all more than 16,000 feet (4,853 m). In addition to the better known peaks, numerous, lesser-known summits have yet to be climbed during a season that runs from April to June, when the snow gets soft.

Spring is the best time for skiing, whether cross-country or downhill. Cross-country skiers often charter ski planes to reach isolated valleys. Downhill skiers essentially use planes as a chair lift. Helicopter landings are not permitted within Wrangell-St. Elias park and preserve but areas of the Chugach Mountains

outside the park are becoming famous for steep, deep heli-skiing. Extreme skiers compete annually for world titles.

Summer is the time for hiking and biking. Within all four parks there are only limited trails near roads. Hiking means mostly a trek across open forests or alpine tundra and stream crossings without bridges. Hikes in the more remote parts of the parks usually involve charter planes for drop-off and/or pickup. Overnight trips in Kluane and Glacier Bay need a backcountry permit. Bear-resistant canisters

Kayakers explore Wolf Point in upper Muir Inlet in Glacier Bay National Park. (Roy Corral)

may be required for food storage. Mountain biking is becoming a popular activity on Kluane and Wrangell-St. Elias trails as well as in dry creek beds.

Whitewater kayaking requires developed skills, but whitewater rafting can be a thrill for all age groups. All four parks have outstanding Class III to Class IV whitewater rivers, with some even more demanding stretches. Trips on the Tatshenshini and Alsek rivers begin in Kluane, traverse Tatshenshini-Alsek Wilderness Provincial Park, and end at Dry Bay in Glacier Bay National Preserve. The Kluane portion of the Alsek River was designated a Canadian Heritage River in 1986. The number of permits to float either river is limited, amounting to one a day during the 100-day season. In Wrangell-St. Elias National Park and Preserve, the Copper and Chitina rivers offer good whitewater opportunities as well as some road access points. For all the parks, local outfitters provide rafting equipment as well as guided trips.

Sea kayaking attracts boaters to Glacier Bay. Bartlett Cove is usually the starting point for a day trip around the Beardslee Islands, several days of paddling up the bay, or boarding the ship Spirit of Adventure for a drop-off on some isolated beach. Glacier Bay may be the only national park that has more kayaks than vehicles. Overnight kayakers need a back-country permit, bear-resistant canisters for food storage, and a brief orientation about bear safety and camping etiquette. The Park Service limits backcountry permits to 2,200 per season.

Glacier Bay is also a popular destination among owners of inboard motorboats. There are, however, a limited number of permits issued and some fiords are off-limits to motorized boats.

Flightseeing has become a favorite, albeit controversial, activity. Charter planes in most communities surrounding the parks offer wilderness tours from the air. The controversy stems from noise created by planes and helicopters that can disturb wildlife and deprive those on the ground of a wilderness experience. Limited ceilings and flight paths have been tried to reduce this problem with mixed results.

Trophy hunting was one of the early draws of the Wrangell and St. Elias mountains. Today trophy hunting continues in the preserve portions of the U.S. parks. In addition, subsistence hunting and fishing are allowed in the U.S. parks/preserves and in portions of the Canadian parks. Although sport fishing is a popular activity in Alaska, not much occurs within the parks because of limited freshwater habitat.

Each of the world heritage parks are wrestling with the problem of accommodating growing numbers of people who want to visit and an increasing number of uses by those who do. Some uses, particularly those that are motorized, can physically or aesthetically alter the pristine qualities of the park. But even hiking can create ruts if trails are not properly located. Mitigating these problems often results in restrictions, which disturbs some users.

Regardless of the increasing presence of people in each of the parks, there still is the opportunity to experience nature on its terms. It is still a place where change is mostly induced by nature.

Mounted on the wall at the Kluane Visitor Reception Centre is a statement about the

Wrangell and St. Elias mountains written by George O. Young, the hunter-turned-conservationist.

We had gone far beyond the beaten trail and looked upon a great wilderness undefaced by the hands of man. I trust that I may be able always to retain in my mind the picture of that wilderness; the majestic mountains and valleys: the yawning chasms; the great rivers and monstrous glaciers which feed them; that I will always keep fresh the memory of the Northern Lights, the azure skies, the glorious sunsets, and the beautiful mountain sheep as they grazed so peacefully on

FACING PAGE:
Wilderness guide Joyce Majiski scales a striated rock face above Lowell Lake in Kluane National Park. (Cathie Archbould)

ABOVE:
A fly fisherman casts into the Tsiu River in the Chugach Mountains east of Cape Yakataga. Although many waterways are clouded by glacial silt and thus of limited value for sport fishing, clear-running streams can offer the angler salmon and an assortment of freshwater fish. (John Hyde/Wild Things)

plots of green or wound their way over lofty crests. One of my greatest hopes is that I may sometime return to that country and again gaze upon its beauties and wonders.

If Young were to return today, 80 years later, he would probably be pleased. There haven't been many human-induced changes within this world heritage wilderness; it remains as wild and natural as he saw it. The challenge for us is to protect this land so that if we were to return in 80 years, we too would find its beauties and wonders intact. ▲

FACING PAGE:
Among the most massive mountains on earth, Mount Logan towers 19,545 feet (5,929 m) in the St. Elias Mountains. Hummingbird Ridge rises on the left in this view taken from Seward Glacier. These backcountry travelers are camped at 5,700 feet (1,729 m). (Brian Okonek)

LEFT:
Mountain climbers are one contingent of adventurers who use the world heritage backcountry. Among the first groups to explore this wilderness, pioneer climbing parties began arriving early in the 20th century, looking for unclimbed peaks and new traverses. Mountain climbing is still popular here, where this pilot and others fly climbers onto Grand Plateau Glacier to explore northern Glacier Bay National Park. (Scott Darsney)

MASTER OF BIG WATER

There is a place where nature at its most primordial waits, where river water flowing at 50,000 cubic feet per second drills past ice and rock. To this place, Turnback Canyon, came Walter Lloyd Blackadar, master of big water.

In the gorge and stranded! This has been a day! I want any other kayaker or would-be expert to read my words well! The Alsek Gorge is unpaddleable!

Walt Blackadar wrote these comments in his diary in August 1971, as he was sitting, exhausted, on a wet bank beside a monumental river. History records that no one else had done what he was doing, paddle Turnback Canyon, the great gorge on the Alsek River, alone, in a kayak.

The Alsek River begins in the Yukon, and winds 240 miles (384 km) to the Gulf of Alaska. About 60 miles (96 km) miles downstream from Haines Junction, the gorge awaits. Running in a channel more than a half-mile wide before entering the canyon, river water is funneled through a slot in places less than 50 feet wide (15 m). Flanked by steep slopes rising a vertical mile on the left side and the massive face of Tweedsmuir Glacier on the right, anyone or anything approaching too close to the canyon's entrance is sucked into a maelstrom. Blackadar compared his run down Turnback to "trying to run down a coiled rattler's back...."

Dr. Walt Blackadar, surgeon, arrived in Salmon, Idaho, in 1949, married, with two small daughters, seeking a fresh start from his New Jersey youth and medical studies at Dartmouth and Columbia. He was looking for "The West;" he envisioned fishing, hunting, physical and mental challenges. His part of the West was replete with wild rivers, and Blackadar took up kayaking as a way to pit his strength against this wilderness. By the end of the 1960s he had become an accomplished boatman and leader of a growing contingent of whitewater kayakers.

After experience on the Colorado River in the Grand Canyon, Blackadar was looking for another challenge as his 49th birthday approached. He told his diary: *I'm not suicidal, but I get depressed watching so many patients with incurable diseases.... I was painfully aware of how fragile life is and I figured... we're all going to die eventually anyway.*

Blackadar had only known of the Alsek River for a short time when he settled on it as his next big adventure. A 1970 article in *Alaska* magazine about a plane crash and the ordeal of the only survivor brought the Alsek to public attention. Blackadar was intrigued. At first he tried to interest others in coming along, but no one would commit. Turnback was reputed to be unrunnable. So the doctor came north on his own.

Four days after leaving his put-in point on the Alsek at Haines Junction, Blackadar approached Tweedsmuir Glacier on August 25. Today he would find out just how

Understandably, Walt Blackadar took no photos of his solo run through Turnback Canyon. This 1976 photo shows the big water kayaker on one of his attempts to run Devil's Gorge on the Susitna River in Southcentral Alaska. In his biography of Blackadar, Ron Watters writes that other kayakers had more technical skill, but few could match the doctor for sheer mental and physical strength in powering a kayak through turbulent water. (John Dondero)

Hikers ascend slopes above the Alsek River near Lowell Glacier and before the river enters Turnback Canyon. (Cathie Archbould)

fragile life could be. In a region of big ice, Tweedsmuir is one of the largest glaciers. Three miles (4.8 km) wide for much of its length, it flares to 10 miles (16 km) along the riverfront. Ron Watters writes in his biography, *Never Turn Back* (1994), that "when Blackadar arrived... the Tweedsmuir was beginning to surge. Ice calves weighing tons fractured off the exposed toe of the glacier and swirled towards the canyon. The ante was upped, the dangers of running Turnback Canyon multiplied."

The canyon seemed to sneak up on Blackadar. He survived the first set of rapids, even though in his own words he did some "foolish" things, like accidentally throwing his paddle beyond reach while trying to find a stable position against a cliff for the paddle, so he could raise himself out of the kayak. By the time he reached the second major hurdle, he was in better control. But what he saw wasn't reassuring: *A huge 45-degree drop of 30 feet or more into a boiling hell*, wrote Blackadar. The doctor had

decided to portage, but nature decided otherwise. Quoting from Blackadar's diary, Watters describes what happened. "He never made the intended portage. Just before he reached the stopping point, his boat was jerked away and caught by a whirlpool." *The boat was sucked by the stern into a perfectly vertical position, then whirled 1-1/2 times around and plopped in upside down. I rolled*

up immediately and easily caught the eddy as planned, but in the wrong place.

"He struggled to get into the necessary position but he judged that the lower end of the eddy where he needed to take out was 10 feet higher than his location on the upstream side of the eddy." Watters continues, "While he was attempting to reach his intended stopping point, the

current caught him again and flung him toward the Boiling Hell. He could not stop now. He had to run it."

Now I knew I had a paddle ahead! Just then an iceberg the size of my bedroom appeared alongside, charging for the drop. I hurriedly turned my boat around and paddled upstream with all my strength while sliding backward into the falls. Missed the iceberg which went

The Alsek River enters Alsek Lake from the upper left and exits at midleft. Alsek Glacier meets the lake at right, as does an arm of Grand Plateau Glacier at lower right. (R.E. Johnson)

against the incredible force of the water, the fiberglass on the left side... ripped. Water poured into the boat, making it heavy and unwieldy. Yet it was the added weight of the water in his boat which finally released him, pushing him far enough under the water to reach downstream current which flushed him out of the reversal."

Blackadar had survived the roller but his boat was damaged. "Now he found himself caught again, this time in the hole below the roller," Watters notes. "He tried four more rolls." *I got scrubbed, tumbled and shaken; rolled and missed — rolled and missed. Finally I caught a breath, calmed my nerves, jammed my knees solidly into the sides of the boat and on my sixth try made a perfect roll and popped up. I found the boat swamped and uncontrollable in the middle of the river. Only the air bladders were keeping it afloat. My body was in water to the armpits, and I was heading for a rapids.... I made*

ahead, flipped and hung upside down while the boat was tossed out of the most violent boils before rolling up.

After more of what he described as a "frothy mess," Blackadar was able to get out on the right bank to scout the next danger. He was tired and hoped the worst was behind him; he was wrong.

Ahead lay a 20-foot (6 m) wave that curled back on itself. Such waves, called rollers, create a reverse current that can trap and kill if a kayaker cannot punch through. Blackadar studied the roller and a hole on the right side just below the wave, and studied some more. None of his options looked promising, all were dangerous and could easily cost him his life. Finally, decision made, he returned to his kayak. All his mental and physical strength were focused on getting through the roller.

"His boat climbed up the huge wave. He reached out with his paddle, trying to propel himself through the wall of water caused by the reversal," Watters writes. "Crashing into the wall, he was stopped dead and violently thrown upside down.... His boat was caught." [I] *could feel the tug of war. The boat bouncing in the roller sideways.* "He tried reaching with his paddle and pulling. Then as he strained *a tremendous effort to force the swamped boat to the shore.... Finally I reached the bank holding onto the kayak by a strap, and as I rolled out on the bank I said 'thanks.'*

Exhausted, Blackadar took out his fiberglass repair kit and began fixing his kayak. As drizzle fell, he also wrote in his diary. *I'm not coming back. Not for $50,000, not for all the tea in China. Read my words well and don't be a fool. It's unpaddleable.* After Turnback Canyon's boiling hell, the rest of the Alsek was just something to get down and out of. Pilot Layton Bennett picked him up at Dry Bay and the doctor flew back to Idaho.

Walt Blackadar went on to new kayaking adventures, including several tries at Devil's Canyon on the Susitna River in Southcentral Alaska. He was featured in nationally televised documentaries, such as American Sportsman, and acted as spokesman for the growing sport of whitewater kayaking at trade shows and other events. He supported environmental causes, pushing for expansion of wilderness designations in Idaho. And he never did come back.

In May 1978, Blackadar, age 55, was leading kayakers down the South Fork of the Payette River in Idaho when a sweeper caught his kayak, holding him underwater until he drowned.

In 1980, the federal government established the River of No Return Wilderness in central Idaho, culmination of a nationwide effort to protect the largest wilderness in the Lower 48, and a cause for which Blackadar fought hard. Watters suggests that although the Alsek was his greatest triumph, the Idaho wilderness may be Blackadar's greatest legacy. Perhaps, but the world heritage wilderness of Alaska and Canada can offer another candidate. On the left side of the Alsek Valley in the stretch between Lowell and Tweedsmuir glaciers rises a 5,000-foot, inverted-bowl-shaped mountain with a jagged top. When Walt Blackadar made his trip through Turnback, the mountain had no name. Today it is officially Mount Blackadar. •

Note: Idaho-based writer Ron Watters has written several books on outdoor recreation. To prepare his biography of Walt Blackadar, Watters had the cooperation of the Blackadar family, who made the doctor's diaries available to him. In 1983, Watters and Walt Blackadar's son, Bob, mounted an expedition to the Alsek. On August 18, Bob became the first person to summit the mountain named for his father.

— *Penny Rennick*

RIGHT: *Sunset illuminates the confluence of the Alsek and Tatshenshini rivers. The Alsek flows through Turnback Canyon before meeting the Tat. (Joyce Majiski)*

FAR RIGHT: *Dwarf fireweed, also called river beauty, and rafters brighten the Alsek Valley. The wide valley through which much of the upper Alsek flows could lull unsuspecting kayakers and rafters into a false sense of security. Little would they know that downriver lies some of the most turbulent whitewater on the continent. (Cathie Archbould)*

GUARDIAN OF LONG LAKE

By Jeannie Woodring

Editor's note: *An Anchorage writer, lifelong Alaskan and wife of George Matz, Jeannie Woodring first met Cliff Collins in 1997.*

On the McCarthy Road near mile 45, where a 3-mile-long (4.8 km) silvery lake winds through thick forests and scores of birds chorus from the treetops, travelers will find what locals call the Long Lake Wildlife Refuge.

If nearby homesteader Cliff Collins has his way, the area will remain a wilderness refuge forever. Born and raised on a Kansas farm, after a stint in Idaho the opportunity to work in a fish cannery drew him north. Collins moved to Cordova in 1939 with his wife, Jewel, where he owned a jewelry store, served as mayor and raised a family. By the 1960s, driven by a need to return to his farming roots and find a little relief from Cordova's year-round rain, Collins found an old 160-acre (64 ha) homestead sitting on Long Lake next to the Copper River & Northwestern Railway tracks, about a dozen miles from McCarthy. The couple

purchased the property in 1961. Because the road to McCarthy hadn't been built yet, the only way they could reach their property was by flying their small plane to the site on summer weekends.

In the mid-1960s, the Collinses began spending the entire summer at the homestead, and they turned the

abandoned railroad station into a comfortable home. Collins planted a huge garden that, under the lengthy Alaska daylight, grew enough vegetables, from strawberries to spinach, to fill a flatbed to take to Cordova, and he caught enough salmon to feed his family through the winter. Collins expanded the

homestead's original 800-foot (247 m) landing strip into a 2,000-foot (607 m) grassy runway to accommodate small planes.

While the Collinses improved their homestead, the State of Alaska began building a road to McCarthy, primarily along the right-of-way of the abandoned railroad. By 1967, a completed 60-mile (96 km) dirt road connecting the Edgerton Highway to McCarthy lured automobile traffic into the area for the first time.

Aware of the increasing number of visitors passing by his wilderness homestead, Collins took steps to preserve the wildlife that thrived in the area. In the late 1970s the Alaska Department of Fish and Game decided it could no longer afford to maintain fish counts on the salmon swimming up the stream that ran through the property to spawn in Long Lake. The

Cliff and Jewel Collins stand before their estate, a pioneer homestead they purchased in the 1960s after several decades of living in Cordova. (George Matz)

A man of nature and peacefulness, Cliff Collins built this home along Long Lake in the Wrangell Mountains. (George Matz)

Collinses took over the annual counting — free of charge. "We do it because we want to," Collins says.

A bird lover all his life, Collins began putting up nesting boxes in 1970 for the violet-green and tree swallows flitting over his property. "I love the swallows because they eat the mosquitoes that eat me," he says, his blue eyes twinkling. In 1984, he got a bird-banding subpermit from the University of Alaska Fairbanks. He banded between 200 and 275 birds each year and sent his meticulous records to the U.S. Department of the Interior. Researchers began finding his banded swallows along their winter migration routes, in warm-weather places like Mexico and Honduras, and reporting the observations to the government.

Through the 1980s and 1990s, as the Collinses cared for the birds, fish and other wildlife around the homestead, McCarthy began to attract more visitors. Tour companies wanted to bring bigger vehicles into the area. Government agencies talked about paving the McCarthy Road. Greater numbers of visitors meant more pressure for expanded recreation, hunting and fishing on places like Long Lake and other private property within Wrangell-St. Elias National Park and Preserve.

To shield his land from the impacts of more people and development, Collins has taken small steps, like putting signs up on the lake asking that boat motors be restricted to 10 horsepower or less. He has also put his land into a 100-year conservation trust. Going into effect when he dies, the trust places a 100-year hold on development of the property.

And, despite the fact that he's 89, Collins still spends his summers on Long Lake with Jewel. His days are full with planting the garden, banding birds and counting fish.

"This lake is a treasure," Collins says. "I am so very interested in things staying like they are." ■

So You Want to Visit

The world heritage wilderness is waiting. But before you go you need to plan, because visiting here is no "walk in the park." Backcountry travel anywhere in Alaska and Canada can be dangerous. Come prepared with proper gear, current survival skills and the latest weather reports.

Travel in Glacier Bay, Kluane and Tatshenshini-Alsek requires permits, so plan carefully. To begin, contact rangers at the various parks for the most up-to-date information.

Wrangell-St. Elias National Park and Preserve
P.O. Box 439
Mile 105.5 Old Richardson Hwy.
Copper Center, AK 99573
(907) 822-7261

Seasonal stations at Chitina: (907) 823-2205
at Slana: (907) 822-5238
at Yakutat: (907) 784-3295

To reach the park, head to Glennallen at the junction of the Glenn and Richardson highways. Go south on the Richardson Highway. Watch for the Park Service Visitor Center. Turn onto the Edgerton Highway to reach Chitina, then cross the Copper River and onto the McCarthy Road to enter the park. Or you can travel the Tok Cutoff between Tok and Glennallen and turn onto the Nabesna Road at Slana.

Kluane National Park and Reserve
P.O. Box 5495
Haines Junction, YT Y0B 1L0
(867) 634-2329 phone
(867) 634-7208 fax

Tatshenshini-Alsek Wilderness Provincial Park
BC Parks, Tatshenshini Office (Seasonal)
P.O. Box 5544
Haines Junction, YT Y0B 1L0
(867) 634-7043 phone
(867) 634-7208 fax

Kluane and Tatshenshini-Alsek parks can be reached from the Alaska and Haines highways. Either travel the Alaska Highway southeast from Tok and Northway toward Haines Junction, or the Haines Highway beginning from Haines on Lynn Canal in Southeast Alaska. Both BC Parks and the National Park Service require permits to raft the Tatshenshini-Alsek rivers. Contact the parks for more information. Guided hikes and other interpretive programs for Kluane are offered by rangers. Sign up at the Visitor Center in Haines Junction. Because of Turnback Canyon, the Alsek River is extremely dangerous and seldom traveled in its entirety. Most rafters follow the "Tat"

Unmatched geology, such as these formations above the Chitistone River valley in the Wrangells, added to the allure that garnered this region world heritage status. (Steve McCutcheon)

Visitors to Kluane must carry bear-resistant cannisters to store food; visitors to Tatshenshini-Alsek park must use fire pans, portable latrines and bear-resistant cannisters. Although the lower Alsek lies within Glacier Bay National Preserve, Glacier Bay rangers will check for compliance with Canadian regulations.

Glacier Bay National Park and Preserve

Superintendent
Glacier Bay National Park and Preserve
Gustavus, AK 99826-0140
(907) 697-2230 phone

Gustavus Visitors Association
P.O. Box 167
Gustavus, AK 99826

It is not possible to drive to the park; visitors must fly or boat here. Gustavus, connected by a 10-mile (16 km) road to park headquarters at Bartlett Cove, is the closest airport. Flights can be arranged from Juneau or other northern Southeast communities. There is transportation from the airport to Bartlett Cove. Contact the Park Service or Gustavus Visitors Association for more information. To reach Gustavus by boat, private ferries run from Juneau to Gustavus. Kayakers sometimes take the Alaska Marine Highway (state) ferry to Hoonah and paddle across Icy Strait to Bartlett Cove, but this can be a difficult crossing. Bear-resistant cannisters for food storage are required within the park.

until it joins the Alsek below the canyon and continue down the combined river to Dry Bay, where they can arrange to be flown back across the mountains to Haines or northwest to Yakutat.

For information on United Nations World Heritage Sites, please check www.unesco.org/whc on the World Wide Web. ▲

GLOSSARY

Benthic: Bottom-dwelling.

Beringia: The Ice-Age landscape that developed when lowlands of Siberia, central Alaska and the Yukon remained unglaciated and the Bering Land Bridge allowed an interchange of flora, fauna and indigenous people between what is now Asia and North America. By the late Pleistocene, Beringia extended from the Mackenzie River in Canada's Yukon to the Lena River in eastern Siberia.

Caldera: Large depressions on the summit of a volcano caused by the withdrawal of magma.

Calving: Calving is a noted aspect of tidewater glaciers that occurs when a large chunk of ice, or a serac, breaks off the face of the glacier, collapsing into the water with a huge crash followed by an upwelling of water that then radiates out as a tidal-wave-sized ripple.

Continental Shelf: An underwater plain of varying width that lies off the coast and connects to a steep slope leading to ocean depths.

Eskers: Gravel deposits where streams formerly flowed beneath a glacier.

Glacial or Isostatic Rebound: This process is known as isostacy and refers to the earth's crust and mantle remaining in balance in response to an increase or decrease of mass on the earth's surface. When glaciers covered the world heritage area, the elevation of that area was depressed. When the glaciers melted, the land rebounded.

Growing-degree-day: The number of growing degrees for a day is the difference between a daily average temperature and a base temperature suitable for plants that grow in the area. The number of growing-degree days is the number of days above that temperature. Gardeners can use this information to determine how successful a certain type of plant will be.

Hanging Glacier: A valley glacier perched high on a mountainside is called a hanging glacier. It can be distinguished by a short U-shaped valley between ridges that ends abruptly on the steep side of a larger U-shaped valley.

Holocene Epoch: 10,000 years ago to present day.

Jokulhlaups: An Icelandic term for glacial outburst floods that usually result from an ice dam break.

Kettles: Depressions caused by melting of stranded blocks of ice.

Loess Soil: The result of fine grinding by Pleistocene glaciers, this glacially milled silt was born by wind and settled into lowlands where it appears as golden-brown soil.

Moraine: A mixed glacial deposit created by or because of direct contact with glacial ice.

Outwash Plain: A broad, alluvial plain composed of glacially eroded material transported by meltwater. The plain begins at the edge of a retreating glacier and may extend for many miles, such as at Dry Bay.

Piedmont Glaciers: Glaciers that fan out at the base of mountains. Malaspina Glacier is a classic example.

Plant Succession: Changes in plant life over time, beginning with bare ground and evolving to a mature forest.

Plate Tectonics: The theory of the continuous motion of the earth's land masses that are riding on great pieces, or plates, of the earth's crust.

Pleistocene Epoch: The epoch of geological time that began more than 2 million years ago and ended about 10,000 to 15,000 years ago and is commonly known as the Great Ice Age.

Successional Vegetation: See plant succession.

Till: Unsorted glacial drift that was deposited by a glacier and was not reworked by water.

Trimline: A sharp boundary line that marks the maximum extent of a glacier. A change in vegetation or a change in color of the bedrock may indicate the line.

Valley Glaciers: A valley glacier begins when overflow ice from an ice cap moves down a mountain valley much like a river. Valley glaciers now occur in only a few parts of North America, the World Heritage Site being the most prominent. Icefields exist where there is a conglomeration of valley glaciers. ■

BIBLIOGRAPHY

Alaska Department of Fish and Game. *Northern Flying Squirrel*. Wildlife Notebook Series. Juneau: State of Alaska, 1994.

Anderson, Cary. *Alaska's Magnificent Eagles* Vol. 24, No. 4, Alaska Geographic. Anchorage: Alaska Geographic Society, 1997.

Connor, Cathy and Daniel O'Haire. *Roadside Geology of Alaska*. Missoula, Mont.: Mountain Press Publishing Co., 1988.

de Laguna, Frederica. *Under Mount St. Elias*. Washington, D.C.: Smithsonian Institution Press, 1972.

Embick, Andrew. *Fast & Cold, A Guide to Alaska Whitewater*. Valdez, Alaska: Valdez Alpine Books, 1994.

Fisher, Robin. *Vancouver's Voyage*. Vancouver, B.C. and Seattle: Douglas & McIntyre and University of Washington Press, 1992.

Hood, Donald W. and Steven T. Zimmerman. *The Gulf of Alaska, Physical Environment and Biological Resources*. Alaska Office: National Oceanic and Atmospheric Administration, 1986.

Hunt, William, R. *Mountain Wilderness*. Anchorage: Alaska Natural History Association, 1996.

Jones, David L., Allan Cox, Peter Coney and Myrl Beck. "The Growth of Western North America." *Scientific American*. pages 70-84. November 1982.

Madsen, Ken and Graham Wilson. *Rivers of the Yukon, A Paddling Guide*. Whitehorse, Yukon: Primrose Publishing, 1989.

Maser, Chris and R. and E. Miles. *The Redesigned Forest*. San Pedro, Calif.: R. and E. Miles, 1988.

Mayo, Lawrence R. "Advance of Hubbard Glacier and Closure of Russell Fiord, Alaska — Environmental Effects and Hazards in the Yakutat Area" in *Geologic Studies in Alaska by the U.S. Geological Survey During 1987*. Fairbanks: U.S. Geological Survey, 1988.

Molnia, Bruce. *Alaska's Glaciers*. Vol. 9, No. 1, Alaska Geographic. Anchorage: Alaska Geographic Society, 1982.

Mowery, Robert A. and John Zasada. *Den Tree Use and Movements of Northern Flying Squirrels in Interior Alaska and Implications for Forest Management*. Presented at the Fish and Wildlife Relationships in Old-Growth Forests Symposium, Juneau, April 1982.

Nelson, Richard. *The Athabaskans: People of the Forest*. Fairbanks: University of Alaska Fairbanks, 1983.

O'Clair, Rita M., Robert H. Armstrong and Richard Carstensen. *The Nature of Southeast Alaska*. Seattle: Alaska Northwest Books, 1992.

Plafker, George and Henry C. Berg, eds. *The Geology of Alaska*, Vol. G-1 of *The Geology of North America*. Boulder, Colo.: The Geological Society of America Inc., 1994.

Quinlan, Susan, Nancy Tankersley and Paul D. Arneson. *A Guide to Wildlife Viewing in Alaska*. Anchorage: Alaska Dept. of Fish and Game, 1983.

Richter, Donald, Danny Rosenkrans and Margaret J. Steigerwald. *Guide to the Volcanoes of the Western Wrangell Mountains, Alaska-Wrangell-St. Elias National Park and Preserve*. U.S. Geological Survey Bulletin 2072. Washington, D.C.: U.S. Geological Survey, 1995.

Turner, Frederick. *Rediscovering America: John Muir In His Times And Ours*. New York: Viking Penguin Inc., 1985.

Viereck, Leslie and Elbert L. Little. *Alaska Trees and Shrubs*. Washington, D.C.: U.S. Government Printing Office, 1972.

Watters, Ron. *Never Turn Back*. Pocatello, Idaho: The Great Rift Press, 1994.

Wells-Gosling, Nancy. *Flying Squirrels; Gliders in the Dark*. Washington, D.C.: Smithsonian Institution Press, 1985.

Young, G.O. *Alaskan Yukon Trophies Won and Lost*. Huntington, WV: Standard Publications Inc., 1947.

INDEX

Ahtna, Lower (Athabaskans) 76, 79, 82, 89
Ahtna Native Corp. 50, 83
Aishihik First Nation 85
Alaska Chilkat Bald Eagle Preserve 4, 54, 58
Alaska Commercial Co. 82
Alaska Native Claims Settlement Act (ANCSA) 83, 84
Alaska National Interest Lands Conservation Act (ANILCA) 83, 84
Alaskan-Yukon Trophies Won and Lost 94
Alexander, Silas 76
Algae 10, 41
Allen, Lt. Henry 89, 91
Alsek River Trail 47
American Sportsman 103
Amphibians 52, 59
Athabaskans 11, 76, 79, 81, 82, 85

Bartlett Cove 23, 41, 42
Bat, little brown 57
Bays
  Disenchantment 25, 78
  Dry 25, 32, 45, 78, 103
  Dundas 25, 42
  Glacier 4, 11, 14, 23, 24, 27, 30, 35, 36, 52, 61, 78, 79, 83, 88, 92, 96
    Boat trips 27, 88, 92
  Lituya 20, 24, 88
  Yakutat 11, 21, 24, 78, 89, 92
Bears
  black 57, 62, 63
  brown/grizzly 52, 56, 57, 62, 64, 65, 67
  glacier 57, 62
Beasley, Rick 82
Beaver 57, 62
Beaver Creek (community) 32, 35
Bennett, Layton 103
Bering, Vitus 11, 48, 81, 85, 90
Beringia 109
Bifelt, Dan 76
Birds 52, 54, 55, 56, 57, 58, 60, 61, 62, 63, 64, 67, 69, 73, 74, 86, 88, 104
Bison 55, 64, 67
Blackadar, Bob 103
Blackadar, Walt 100-103
Boggs, Keith 2
Boreal forest 40, 55

Burwash Landing 32

Cahill, Adrianna 41
Campbell, Robert 89
Caribou 10, 52, 55, 64, 67, 79
Carmack, George 90
Cash economy 82, 83, 85
Champagne First Nation 85
Chilkat blankets 81
Chilkat-Chilkoot (Tlingit) 79, 81, 89
Chipmunk, least 63
Chisana 11, 19, 90
Chitina 4, 21, 49, 50, 51
Chugach Alaska Corp. 83
Chugach Eskimo 79
Chugach Mountains 8, 12, 16, 19, 21, 23, 25, 31, 32, 95, 97
Climate 8, 10, 12, 14, 28-35, 36, 39, 44
  coldest temperature 30
  growing conditions for plants 35
  highest barometric pressure 31
  wettest place 8, 28
  three climate zones 28, 33
Collins, Cliff and Jewel 104-105
Coney, Peter 16
Convention Concerning the Protection of the World Cultural and Natural Heritage 7
Cook, Capt. James 42, 88
Coolidge, President Calvin 50
Cooper, William 50
Copper Oar rafting company 2
Copper River & Northwestern Railway 90, 104
Copper River Delta Critical Habitat Area 4
Cordova 4, 23, 32, 35, 90, 104
Corral, Ben and Hannah 50
Cougar 64
Coyote 55, 67
Cross Sound 28, 54, 61

Dall, William 89
Dalton Post 44
Dalton Trail 90
Deer
  mule 64
  Sitka black-tailed 54, 57
de Laguna, Frederica 81
Di Savoia, Luigi Amedeo 92

Dunn, Robert 92

Earthquakes 12, 20
Ecological Society of America 50
Eichenlaub, Bill 22
Elder, Carolyn 2
Excursion Inlet 67
Eyak 11, 76, 79, 83, 85

Fairweather 14
First Nations 84, 85
First people 76-85
Fish 54, 55, 58, 59, 60, 65, 68, 76, 79, 84
Fishing 67, 80, 82, 97
  commercial 62
Forest, clearcutting 39, 50, 74
Forest, old-growth, 38
Fossil wood 43, 88
Fox, red 55, 67
Freese, Lloyd 2
Fungi *see* mushrooms
Fur seals 54

Getchell, Annie 49
Giardia 63
Glaciation 12, 14, 21-27
  extent 25
Glacier Bay National Park/ Preserve 4, 22, 32, 36, 38, 43-45, 60, 84, 85, 95
Glaciers 12
  Alsek 102
  Bering 8, 23, 31
  Gilman 14
  Grand Pacific 24
  Grand Plateau 99, 102
  Hubbard 8, 21, 25
  Johns Hopkins 27
  Kennicott 23, 90
  LaPerouse 24
  Lowell 10, 25, 48, 65, 101, 103, 104
  Malaspina 8, 23, 89, 90
  Margerie 46, 61
  Muir 4
  Nabesna 8
  Nizina 12
  Riggs 4, 50
  Russell 89
  Seward 99
  Tweedsmuir 100, 101, 103
  Variegated 24
Glennallen 32, 35, 40, 49, 50, 67
Goat, mountain 10, 56, 57, 62, 67

Gulkana 35
Gustavus 32
Gustavus Visitor Association 108

Haines 4
Haines Junction 32, 35, 64, 100
Hare, snowshoe 57, 62
Harriman Alaska Expedition 88, 92
Harriman, Edward H. 92
Harrison, Will 24
Highways
  Alaska 32, 46, 47, 64
  Edgerton 49, 50, 104
  Haines 44, 47
  McCarthy Road 50, 51, 91, 104
  Richardson 50
Holocene epoch 22, 109
Hoonah 78, 79, 83, 84, 108
Hostetter, Kristin 49
Hudson's Bay Co. 89
Hunting 92, 97

Ice, blue color 27
Icefield Range 17, 46, 95
Icefields 4, 8
  Bagley 8, 23
Iceworms 10, 56
Icy Strait 25, 61, 83
Insects 54
Islands
  Beardslee group 96
  Kayak 86, 88
  Kidney 43
  Marble 61
  Osier 21
  Russell 89
Invertebrates, marine 67, 80, 82

Jarvis, Jon 2
Jimmie, Charlie Sr. 81

Kennecott (community) 23, 94
Kennicott, Robert 23
Kluane First Nation 85
Kluane National Park 2, 4, 7, 10, 16, 23, 25, 27, 30, 36, 39, 67, 84, 85, 95
Klukshu 84

Lakes
  Alsek 48, 102
  Grizzly 49
  Kathleen 16, 65
  Kenny 50
  Kluane 21, 64, 65
  Lowell 97
  Tebay 4

Vitus 31
Lakina Valley 2, 30
La Perouse, Cmdr. Jean Francois de Galaup de 88
Landscape, human presence on 7, 11
Landslides 20, 21
Little Ice Age 22, 23, 25, 42
Lipkin, Rob 2
London, Jack 30
Long Lake Wildlife Refuge 104
Lynx 57, 62, 67

Mackenzie, Alexander 88
Magnetic orientation of rocks 17
Majiski, Joyce 97
Malaspina, Alessandro 25
Maps 6, 33
Marks, Mrs. 81
Marmot, hoary 56, 57, 62
Marten, pine 57, 62, 73
Marvin, Harry 83
Matz, George 1, 2, 4, 104
McCarthy 2, 12, 28, 32, 35, 49, 50, 51, 91, 94
McCrae, Gordon 2
Mentasta Mountains 32
Mice 57, 62
Migration, animal 57-60
Mining 90, 91
Mink 57, 62
Mitchell, Carl 2
Moieties 80
Moose 10, 44, 55, 57, 67, 79
Moss, Mary Beth 2, 60
Mount
  Blackadar 103
  Blackburn 50, 95
  Bona 95
  Castle Mountain 50
  Chitistone Mountain 12
  Churchill 19
  Drum 19, 49
  Everest 8
  Goatherd Mountain 16
  Lituya Mountain 27
  Logan 8, 11, 92, 95, 99
  Nelson Mountain 21
  Sanford 95
  Sheep Mountain 64
  St. Elias 8, 11, 28, 86, 89, 92, 95
  Whitney 8
  Wrangell 4, 19, 92
Mountain climbing 92, 99
Mountains, highest 8, 11
Mowery, Robert 74
Mozen, Howard 2
Muir Inlet 4
Muir, John 4, 14, 27, 41, 43, 88, 89, 92

Mushrooms 70, 71, 72, 74
Muskrat 57

Nabesna 19, 91
Nabesna Mine 49, 91
Nabesna Road 19, 49
NaDene 76
Nelson, Richard 79, 81
Nepal, comparison with 8
Never Turn Back 101
Nixon, Richard 7
Northway 32, 35
Northwest Territories, provisional district of 90
Nutzotin Mountains 8, 59

Octopus 82
Oregon Climate Center 28
Otters
  river 57, 62
  sea 61, 81, 82, 86

Pacific Coast Steamship Co. 89, 92
Pika, collared 56, 57
Plate tectonics 12-21
  chart of composite terranes 15
Pleistocene epoch 21, 22, 24, 48, 109
Porcupine 57, 62
Porpoises
  Dall's 61
  harbor 61
Rain forest, Pacific 36, 38, 42, 54, 76
Rebound, glacial or isostatic 21, 23, 109
Recreation, outdoor 10, 44, 92-108
Reptiles 52, 58
River of No Return Wilderness 103
River rafting 44-45
Rivers
  Alsek 10, 21, 22, 25, 32, 35, 36, 44, 45, 47, 48, 52, 62, 65, 78, 81, 85, 96, 100-103
  Chilkat 54, 58
  Chisana 76
  Chitina 21, 30, 32, 40, 67
  Chitistone 108
  Copper 4, 19-22, 28, 31, 36, 47, 49, 52, 58, 76, 79, 81-83, 86, 89, 91, 96
  Dezadeash 47
  Kennicott 94
  Kluane 65
  Nabesna 76
  Nisling 64
  Situk 21

Slims 24, 30,
  Tatshenshini 44, 45, 63,90
    rafting on 44, 62, 63
  Tsiu 97
  Yukon 21
Rosenkrans, Danny 2, 14, 92
Russell Fiord 21, 25, 89
Russell, Israel Cook 89
Russian American Co. 82

Sealaska Corp. 84
Sea lion, Steller 61, 62, 68, 78
Seals
  harbor 61, 68, 78, 79
  northern elephant 54
  northern fur 54, 86
Seaweed succession 41, 60
Service, Robert 30, 31
Shakwak Trench 47, 65
Sheep
  Dall 52, 56, 62-65, 67, 79
  stone 62
Sheep Mountain Visitor Centre 64
Shellfish 60, 61
Shrews 57, 62
Skookum Jim 90
Simpson, Greg 30
Skolai Creek 8
Slana 19, 32
Snag Creek 30
Splash wave 20
Spruce bark beetle 47, 50, 51, 57
Squirrels
  arctic ground 56, 57
  northern flying 57, 64, 69-75
  red 57, 69, 70, 72, 73
St. Elias Mountains 8, 12, 14, 16, 17, 19, 21, 25, 28, 30-32, 36, 41, 45, 46, 64, 78, 91, 99
Steller, George W. 86
Steller's sea cow 88
Strelna 49
Surging glaciers 24

Tagish (Dawson) Charlie 90
Tanana, Upper (Athabaskans) 76
Tatshenshini-Alsek Wilderness Provincial Park 4, 7, 32, 47, 84, 85, 96
Taylor, George 28
Tetlin National Wildlife Refuge 59
The Athabaskans: People of the Boreal Forest 79
Tlingits 11, 76, 78-83, 85, 88, 89
Tok Cutoff 49
Tourism 89, 92, 95

Trading with Westerners 81, 82, 88, 91
Tree line, definition 39
Truffles see mushrooms
Turnback Canyon 100-103, 106
Tutchone, Southern (Athabaskans) 76, 81

Under Mount St. Elias: The History and Culture of the Yakutat Tlingit 81
United Nations Educational, Scientific and Cultural Organization (UNESCO) 7
United States, purchase of Alaska 89

Vancouver, Capt. George 90
Vegetation 10, 35-51, 72-75
  five general types 39
  Glacier Bay 41-43
  Kluane 45-48
  old-growth forest 38
  plant succession 36, 43, 50, 109
  Tatshenshini-Alsek 43-45
  Wrangell-St. Elias 48-51
Volcanoes 19
Voles 57, 62, 64

Watters, Ron 100-103
Weasels 54, 57, 62, 73
  short-tailed 64
Western Hemisphere Shore-bird Reserve Network 58
Wetlands 59
Whales
  fin 54
  gray 54
  humpback 52, 54, 57, 61
  killer 52, 54, 61
  minke 54, 61
White River Ash Bed 19
Wildlife 52-68
  Glacier Bay 60-62
  Kluane 63-65
  Tatshenshini-Alsek 62-63
  Wrangell-St. Elias 65-68
Witches broom 71, 72
Wolverine 56, 62, 67
Wolves 56, 62, 67
Woodchuck 63, 64
Woodring, Jeannie 104
World Heritage Site 7, 12, 15
  size 4, 20
  components 20
  highest point 20
  major rivers 20
  major glaciers 20
  tree line 20
Wrangell Mountains 2, 4, 8, 12, 14, 16, 19, 21, 25, 30-

32, 39, 41, 49, 89-92, 104, 105, 108
Wrangell-St. Elias National Park/Preserve 4, 7, 8, 14, 36, 84, 91

Yakataga seismic gap 20
Yakutat 21, 32, 35, 78, 82, 84, 86, 90
Yerxa, Rusty 2
Young, George O. 94, 97, 99

Zasada, John 74

Photographers

Anchorage Municipal Libraries: 90
Archbould, Cathie: 37, 96, 101, 103
Baker, Bruce H.: 44
Butterfield, Bob: 23, 66
Cahill, Matthew: 14, 41, 46, 60, 82
Corral, Roy: 30, 50, 95
Croll, Scott: 22, 42, 43, 59, 62, 67, 93
Cross Fox Photography: 1, 30, 64
Darack, Ed: 17
Darsney, Scott: 99
Dick, Laurent: 5, 28, 44
Dondero, John: 100
Franke, Vince: 48
Goodman, Roz: 19
Grace, Jim: 69, 70, 71, 72, 73, 74, 75
Harriman Alaska Expedition: 78 (2), 79, 88
Herning-Wickens, Colleen: 77
Hyde, John: 25, 27, 31, 53, 54, 55, 56, 63, 65, 68, 80, 97
Johnson, R.E.: 34, 87, 102
Lotscher, Chlaus: 58
Majiski, Joyce: 103, 107
Matz, George: 10, 16, 22, 32, 38, 40, 84, 85, 104, 105
McCutcheon, Steve: 21, 108
Metzler, Curvin: 13, 94
Nickles, Jon R.: 91
Okonek, Brian: 98
Salisbury, Kate: 49
Sherwonit, Bill: 9, 47
Smith, Corinne: 57
Speaks, Michael: 10, 16, 24
Staff: 81, 83
U.S. Geological Survey: 89
Villeneuve, Mario: cover, 26
Woodring, Jeannie: back cover
Wuerthner, George: 3, 35, 39, 51, 61, 68

ALASKA GEOGRAPHIC. Back Issues

The North Slope, Vol. 1, No. 1. Out of print.
One Man's Wilderness, Vol. 1, No. 2. Out of print.
Admiralty...Island in Contention, Vol. 1, No. 3. $19.95.
Fisheries of the North Pacific, Vol. 1, No. 4. Out of print.
Alaska-Yukon Wild Flowers, Vol. 2, No. 1. Out of print.
Richard Harrington's Yukon, Vol. 2, No. 2. Out of print.
Prince William Sound, Vol. 2, No. 3. Out of print.
Yakutat: The Turbulent Crescent, Vol. 2, No. 4. Out of print.
Glacier Bay: Old Ice, New Land, Vol. 3, No. 1. Out of print.
The Land: Eye of the Storm, Vol. 3, No. 2. Out of print.
Richard Harrington's Antarctic, Vol. 3, No. 3. $19.95.
The Silver Years, Vol. 3, No. 4. $19.95.
Alaska's Volcanoes, Vol. 4, No. 1. Out of print.
The Brooks Range, Vol. 4, No. 2. Out of print.
Kodiak: Island of Change, Vol. 4, No. 3. Out of print.
Wilderness Proposals, Vol. 4, No. 4. Out of print.
Cook Inlet Country, Vol. 5, No. 1. Out of print.
Southeast: Alaska's Panhandle, Vol. 5, No. 2. Out of print.
Bristol Bay Basin, Vol. 5, No. 3. Out of print.
Alaska Whales and Whaling, Vol. 5, No. 4. $19.95.
Yukon-Kuskokwim Delta, Vol. 6, No. 1. Out of print.
Aurora Borealis, Vol. 6, No. 2. $19.95.
Alaska's Native People, Vol. 6, No. 3. Out of print.
The Stikine River, Vol. 6, No. 4. $19.95.
Alaska's Great Interior, Vol. 7, No. 1. $19.95.
Photographic Geography of Alaska, Vol. 7, No. 2. Limited.
The Aleutians, Vol. 7, No. 3. Out of print.
Klondike Lost, Vol. 7, No. 4. Out of print.
Wrangell-Saint Elias, Vol. 8, No. 1. Limited.
Alaska Mammals, Vol. 8, No. 2. Out of print.
The Kotzebue Basin, Vol. 8, No. 3. Out of print.

Alaska National Interest Lands, Vol. 8, No. 4. $19.95.
Alaska's Glaciers, Vol. 9, No. 1. Revised 1993. $19.95.
Sitka and Its Ocean/Island World, Vol. 9, No. 2. Limited.
Islands of the Seals: The Pribilofs, Vol. 9, No. 3. $19.95.
Alaska's Oil/Gas & Minerals Industry, Vol. 9, No. 4. $19.95.
Adventure Roads North, Vol. 10, No. 1. $19.95.
Anchorage and the Cook Inlet Basin, Vol. 10, No. 2. $19.95.
Alaska's Salmon Fisheries, Vol. 10, No. 3. $19.95.
Up the Koyukuk, Vol. 10, No. 4. $19.95.
Nome: City of the Golden Beaches, Vol. 11, No. 1. $19.95.
Alaska's Farms and Gardens, Vol. 11, No. 2. $19.95.
Chilkat River Valley, Vol. 11, No. 3. $19.95.
Alaska Steam, Vol. 11, No. 4. $19.95.
Northwest Territories, Vol. 12, No. 1. $19.95.
Alaska's Forest Resources, Vol. 12, No. 2. $19.95.
Alaska Native Arts and Crafts, Vol. 12, No. 3. $24.95.
Our Arctic Year, Vol. 12, No. 4. $19.95.
Where Mountains Meet the Sea, Vol. 13, No. 1. $19.95.
Backcountry Alaska, Vol. 13, No. 2. $19.95.
British Columbia's Coast, Vol. 13, No. 3. $19.95.
Lake Clark/Lake Iliamna, Vol. 13, No. 4. Out of print.
Dogs of the North, Vol. 14, No. 1. $21.95.
South/Southeast Alaska, Vol. 14, No. 2. Limited.
Alaska's Seward Peninsula, Vol. 14, No. 3. $19.95.
The Upper Yukon Basin, Vol. 14, No. 4. $19.95.
Glacier Bay: Icy Wilderness, Vol. 15, No. 1. Limited.
Dawson City, Vol. 15, No. 2. $19.95.
Denali, Vol. 15, No. 3. $19.95.
The Kuskokwim River, Vol. 15, No. 4. $19.95.
Katmai Country, Vol. 16, No. 1. $19.95.
North Slope Now, Vol. 16, No. 2. $19.95.
The Tanana Basin, Vol. 16, No. 3. $19.95.
The Copper Trail, Vol. 16, No. 4. $19.95.
The Nushagak Basin, Vol. 17, No. 1. $19.95.
Juneau, Vol. 17, No. 2. Limited.
The Middle Yukon River, Vol. 17, No. 3. $19.95.
The Lower Yukon River, Vol. 17, No. 4. $19.95.
Alaska's Weather, Vol. 18, No. 1. $19.95.
Alaska's Volcanoes, Vol. 18, No. 2. $19.95.
Admiralty Island: Fortress of Bears, Vol. 18, No. 3. $21.95.
Unalaska/Dutch Harbor, Vol. 18, No. 4. $19.95.
Skagway: A Legacy of Gold, Vol. 19, No. 1. $19.95.
Alaska: The Great Land, Vol. 19, No. 2. $19.95.
Kodiak, Vol. 19, No. 3. Out of print.
Alaska's Railroads, Vol. 19, No. 4. $19.95.
Prince William Sound, Vol. 20, No. 1. $19.95.
Southeast Alaska, Vol. 20, No. 2. $19.95.
Arctic National Wildlife Refuge, Vol. 20, No. 3. $19.95.
Alaska's Bears, Vol. 20, No. 4. $19.95.
The Alaska Peninsula, Vol. 21, No. 1. $19.95.
The Kenai Peninsula, Vol. 21, No. 2. $19.95.
People of Alaska, Vol. 21, No. 3. $19.95.

Prehistoric Alaska, Vol. 21, No. 4. $19.95.
Fairbanks, Vol. 22, No. 1. $19.95.
The Aleutian Islands, Vol. 22, No. 2. $19.95.
Rich Earth: Alaska's Mineral Industry, Vol. 22, No. 3. $19.95.
World War II in Alaska, Vol. 22, No. 4. $19.95.
Anchorage, Vol. 23, No. 1. $21.95.
Native Cultures in Alaska, Vol. 23, No. 2. $19.95.
The Brooks Range, Vol. 23, No. 3. $19.95.
Moose, Caribou and Muskox, Vol. 23, No. 4. $19.95.
Alaska's Southern Panhandle, Vol. 24, No. 1. $19.95.
The Golden Gamble, Vol. 24, No. 2. $19.95.
Commercial Fishing in Alaska, Vol. 24, No. 3. $19.95.
Alaska's Magnificent Eagles, Vol. 24, No. 4. $19.95.
Steve McCutcheon's Alaska, Vol. 25, No. 1. $21.95.
Yukon Territory, Vol. 25, No. 2. $21.95.
Climbing Alaska, Vol. 25, No. 3. $21.95.
Frontier Flight, Vol. 25, No. 4. $21.95. Our 100th Issue!
Restoring Alaska: Legacy of an Oil Spill, Vol. 25, No. 3. $21.95.

PRICES AND AVAILABILITY SUBJECT TO CHANGE

Membership in The Alaska Geographic Society includes a subscription to *ALASKA GEOGRAPHIC®*, the Society's colorful, award-winning quarterly.

Call or write for current membership rates or to request a free catalog. *ALASKA GEOGRAPHIC®* back issues are also available (see above list). **NOTE:** This list was current in mid-1999. If more than a year or two has elapsed since that time, contact us before ordering to check prices and availability of back issues, particularly books marked Limited.

When ordering back issues please add $4 for the first book and $2 for each additional book ordered for Priority Mail. Inquire for non-U.S. postage rates. To order, send check or money order (U.S. funds) or VISA/MasterCard information (including expiration date and your phone number) with list of titles desired to:

ALASKA GEOGRAPHIC.

P.O. Box 93370 • Anchorage, AK 99509-3370
Phone: (907) 562-0164 • Fax (907) 562-0479

ALASKA GEOGRAPHIC.
Notecard Set
$12.95
(+ $3.50 shipping/handling)

Each set includes 12 blank cards with envelopes, three cards each of four popular images from the cover of ALASKA GEOGRAPHIC®. Order from:

Alaska Geographic Society
P.O. Box 93370, Anchorage AK 99509-3370
907-562-0164; fax 907-562-0479; e-mail akgeo@aol.com

NEXT ISSUE: VOL. 26, No. 3
The Bering Sea
What's wrong with the Bering Sea? This ecosystem, whose productivity is world renowned, has suffered in recent years and no one is certain why. This issue delves into the physical environment of the sea, the mammals, fish and birds that contribute to its productivity, and the people whose livelihood depends on its health. To members, summer 1999.